PASTORAL MUSIC
IN PRACTICE
5

The Pastoral Musician

Edited by Virgil C. Funk

The Pastoral Press
Washington, D.C.

ISBN: 0-912405-76-7

The Pastoral Press
225 Sheridan Street, NW
Washington, D.C. 20011
(202) 723-1254

The Pastoral Press is the publications division of the National
Association of Pastoral Musicians, a membership organization of
musicians and clergy dedicated to fostering the art of musical
liturgy.

Printed in the United States of America

CONTENTS

INTRODUCTION

One of the many fruits of the Second Vatican Council has been a focus on ministry, on the members of the church serving one another. Not that such service did not exist in the preconciliar church, but today it is seen as being integral to our very understanding of what it means to be the Body of Christ, to be members of a community whose identity is rooted in having been baptized into Christ. The church is a servant church. All its members are called to service, whether in specifically designated ways or—as is true of all of us—as being people who endeavor to follow the path laid out for us by Jesus, the Jesus who came to be the servant of others.

At no time is the vision of service more evident than when the community gathers to proclaim—in symbol, word, and song—its praise of the Father. If worship was formerly considered the task of a priest who did sacred things for a watching congregation, today we know that worship involves a wide complexus of ministerial role, of people serving one another and being served by one another. Thus we have, in addition to ordained ministries, such lay ministries as those of reader, acolyte, eucharistic minister, cantor, choir, and the like. But one of the most important of these lay services is that of the pastoral musician. The reason is simple. The church's liturgy is sung prayer, and the quality of this prayer hinges on the unique ministry of the pastoral musician. All the good will in the world will not bring about a singing assembly if a community lacks pastoral musicians, people whose primary ministry is to enable the community's sung prayer.

The skills demanded of the pastoral musician are indeed numerous: artistic, liturgical, pedagogical, motivational—to mention just a few. The musician is called to be a person of prayer, a person dedicated to excellence, a person committed to the values and aspirations of the community that is served. Since ministries do not exist in isolation one from another, the musician works not alone but in concert with all other ministers in the community. Their common goal is neither self-aggrandizement nor mutual flattery, but to enable the community to become that which it is called to be by baptism—a people following in the footsteps of the Lord and joining the same Lord in joyous praise of the Father.

This volume, containing articles that originally appeared in *Pastoral Music*, is intended to nurture and encourage the vitally important ministry of the pastoral musician. The authors present neither packaged recipes nor facile solutions. Rather, they sketch a vision and offer practical insights so that those exercising this ministry might continue to grow as servants of the sung prayer of the community.

Virgil C. Funk

THE VISION

Nathan Mitchell

ONE

THE MUSICIAN AS MINISTER

In the year 1747, at the age of sixty-three, Johann Sebastian Bach made a journey to the court of King Frederick of Prussia at Postdam. Actually, old Bach didn't care a fig about the king; he had gone to Potsdam to visit one of his many talented sons, Carl Philip Emmanuel, who had become Kapellmeister at Frederick's court. It seems, however, that when the Bach-mobile roared into town, some of Frederick's musical cronies caught wind of it—and before old Bach could even change out of his traveling costume, he was whisked off, periwig and all, to the palace. Frederick wanted the old man to improvise a few trifles on his new Silbermann piano. (Frederick, incidentally, was one of those rare musical monarchs who enjoyed being in the *avant garde* of Europe's cultural life; he correctly predicted that the pianoforte would become the hottest item since sackbutts and rebecs.) In any case, Bach obliged the king by improvising fugues in four, five, and six parts. And just to show everybody who was really the boss, Bach then asked Frederick to give him a fugue subject of the king's own making on which to improvise. The king promptly tossed off a complicated, chromatic little tune in C minor—and Bach astonished everyone present by improvising a perfect fugue right on the spot.

After Bach got back home to Leipzig, he wrote an extremely oily and ingratiating letter to Frederick (after all, Bach's boy worked for the king), and enclosed a set of compositions—chiefly canons and ricercari—based on the tune Frederick himself had composed. Bach called the set *Das musikalische Opfer*, "The Musical Offering." The canons and fugues of "The Musical Offering" are an ingenious *tour de force* of eighteenth-century contrapuntal technique. Bach does everything imaginable with Frederick's chromatic tune: he slows it down, he speeds it up, he turns it upside down, he runs it backward, he chases it around the circle of fifths. But there is one canon in "The Musical Offering" that is particularly spectacular. Bach called it *Canon a due per tonos* (a canon in two voices through [all] the keys)—and he wrote a clever little Latin phrase at the top of the canon: *Ascendenteque modulatione ascendat Gloria Regis* ("As the modulation ascends, so may the Glory of the King ascend!"). Bach was a sly old fox—and this little canon shows just how sly he could be. The canon begins in the key of C minor, but by the time you get to the end of the first canonic imitation, you discover that somehow, some way, Bach has managed to modulate up to the key of D minor. The same thing happens again: you're running along pleasantly in the key of D minor when all of a sudden you get to the end of the second canonic imitation and discover that you're now in the key of E minor. And for the life of you, you can't figure out how you got there. And that's not all: Bach keeps the canonic structure absolutely, perfectly intact. It is a perfect canon at the fifth, which somehow manages to modulate through all the keys—C minor, D minor, E minor, F minor, etc.—until the piece ends right back in the key of C minor, where it all started.

What that old fox Johann Sebastian Bach had given the king was an endlessly rising canon that could, theoretically, go on forever—stretch all the way to musical infinity. And paradoxically, through a series of strange musical loops, Bach manages to destroy our sense of beginnings and endings: the music begins where it ends and ends where it begins. Like the symbolic circle that seems to have neither beginning nor ending, Bach has given us, in his "endlessly rising canon,"a musical image of infinity, a musical paradox of infinite possibilities.

This story of Bach's trip to Postdam—and the music that resulted from his journey—reveals something profound about the relation between musical art and the human hunger for infinity, for transcendence, for what Christians would call "the vision of God." It tells us, among other things, that the human search for God is an endlessly rising canon that begins where it ends. This

probably sounds paradoxical—and it should. The human journey toward God—and God's journey toward us—is a paradox,
an intricate fugue that brings us, at the end, back to the beginning. Perhaps the poet T.S. Eliot said it best in the last of his Four
Quartets.

> What we call the beginning is often the end
> And to make an end is to make a beginning.
> The end is where we start from . . .
> Every phrase and every sentence is an end and a beginning.
> Every poem an epitaph. And any action
> Is a step to the block, to the fire, down the sea's throat
> Or to an illegible stone: and that is where we start.
> We die with the dying:
> See, they depart, and we go with them.
> We are born with the dead:
> See, they return, and they bring with them . . .
> We shall not cease from exploration
> And the end of all our exploring
> Will be to arrive where we started
> And know the place for the first time.

—"Little Gidding," Section V

"The end of all our exploring/ Will be to arrive where we
started/ And know the place for the first time." Both Eliot and
Bach are telling us—one through the medium of language, the
other through the medium of music—that the human hunger for
God is as infinite, and as intricate, as art. Artists are, in fact, the
people who confront us most uncompromisingly with the "paradox of infinity." And for this reason, artists are perhaps our
surest guides on the journey toward God.

THE MUSICIAN: A MYSTAGOGUE

The specific topic at hand is the ministry of one special group
of artists in the Christian community: the musicians—those
much-maligned, much-misunderstood merry-makers who help
us hear what God sounds like. First, the musician's ministry in
the church can be summarized in a single word: *mystagogue*. A
mystagogue is not an insect, nor is it the name of a fatal disease,
nor is it an aphrodisiac like amyl nitrite. A mystagogue is simply

a human being who initiates other human beings into mystery—
a person who guides us in our search for beauty ever ancient and
ever new. Every musician is a mystagogue who uses the symbols
of sound to reveal something new and beautiful about the holy
God who hears. As mystagogue, the musician confronts us with
the paradox of infinity; stretches our imagination about God; and
leads us through the strange labyrinthine loops of an endlessly
rising canon that carries us deeper and deeper into mystery. If it
is still unclear what a mystagogue is, think of Bach: he was and
remains the musical mystagogue *par excellence.*

Like all ministers, musicians help us discover new ways to
explore old mysteries. But this isn't as easy a task as it may
appear. For centuries, traditional Catholic theology has assumed
that the surest path to God is the one that leads through the
discursive reasoning power of human intellect. God is, above all,
a mind—a supremely gifted intelligence, overwhelming in its
breadth and depth, razor-sharp in its power to discern true from
false, virtue from vice. In short, we have been conditioned to
believe that God is a cosmic Intellect, and that human intellects
(however feeble and fallible they may be) are the best examples
of God's image in us. This has been, in fact, the fundamental
tenor of western theology ever since Augustine appealed to the
operations of human will and intellect as a source for understanding God's own trinitarian life.

Where does this leave the artist? At the bottom of the pile,
usually. The church has often regarded artists as people whose
minds and morals are too weak to serve as secure models for
theology or Christian life. It is as though becoming an artist were
slightly indecent, immoral—or at any rate, imperfect. Perhaps it
is for this that we have hundreds of canonized theologians, but
we still don't recognize St. Ludwig van Beethoven, St. Franz
Schubert, St. Pierluigi da Palestrina, or St. Antonio Vivaldi. After
nearly two millennia, the church is still reluctant to accept the
ministry and the theology of the musician.

It is necessary to explore some of the unique gifts the ministry
of musician brings to the Christian assembly. Clearly, there is a
distinctive spirituality for artistic persons in the church—and it is
this spirituality that shapes our pastoral ministry for and among

people. So the first thing is to outline a "spirituality for Christian artists." This will lead to some conclusions about the mystagogic ministry of the musician.

A SPIRITUALITY FOR ARTISTS

Artists are very easy to admire—and also very easy to dislike. Artists are, after all, the militant revolutionaries, the guerrilla warriors of the human psyche; and a church that admires discipline and uniformity finds it difficult to accommodate them. Besides, artists have a disconcerting tendency to play by their own rules: they ambush us with unaccustomed ways of seeing, hearing, and feeling: they pry deep into our sensibilities; they smoke us out of the caves and force us to look straight in the light. We don't like that. We don't like people who are both supremely gifted and supremely mad. But that's what art is: a passionate, seductive madness that grips us in the way blackjack grips a gambler. We leave the artistic experience feeling simultaneously guilty and purified, like thieves who have stolen fire from the gods. Is it any wonder that Plato thought poets and musicians were too much for the Republic to handle?

Outlined below are some elements of a spirituality that embraces both the madness and the giftedness of artistic people in the church. Such a spirituality is neither easy to identify nor simple to describe. For one thing, what often passes for Christian spirituality is little more than cultural garbage liberally sanitized by quotations from the Bible. If this remark seems ungenerous, chalk it up to my experience as a seminary professor. It isn't everywhere that you can hear Gail Sheehy's mandatory mid-life crisis and John's account of Jesus' passion talked about as though they were consubstantial and co-eternal. Nor is it everywhere that you can hear self-help, self-growth, and self-awareness spoken of with the hushed reverence once reserved for theological discussions of the Trinity. But let that pass. As I understand it, art is not the same thing as therapy—nor is spirituality the same thing as transcendental self-attention. An artist is neither an emotional cripple who needs help, nor a degenerate sinner who needs absolution. An artist is simply a crazy, gifted person who is godlike because God too is crazy and gifted: crazy enough to fall in love with human beings—and gifted enough to transform that messy relationship into a perfect work of art called Jesus Christ.

To speak about a spirituality for artists and designers is thus to speak about a Christian way of life for people who are crazy, gifted, and godlike. It is to talk of falling in love with the things of earth—with color, shape, sound, form, texture, water, dirt, stones, trees, and (above all) people. It is to speak about the way a brook-pebbled surface interacts with sunlight on a late afternoon in the middle of April. It is to speak about the geometry of prayer in a twelfth-century Cistercian church so sensitive to sound that a pin dropped in its nave creates a full set of harmonic overtones. It is to speak about symbols so exquisite that they signal simply by being themselves—simply by being bread and salt, water and wine, oil and musk. It is to speak, paradoxically, about the visible colors of music and about the tangible warmth of burnished copper and natural oak. It is to speak, as the American composer John Cage does, of quartets for heartbeat, bulldozer, landslide, and prepared piano.

Falling in Love with the "Impure Poetry" of This Earth

The first element of a Christian spirituality for artists, then, is the process of falling in love—like God—with the "impure poetry" of this earth. The impure poetry of earth was the recurring theme of Pablo Neruda, the Chilean writer and political Marxist who was also Thomas Merton's favorite poet. At first blush, there is something intensely incongruous about this affection between Merton the Christian monk and Neruda the confessed Marxist. But if you think about it for a moment, the incongruity vanishes. Both Merton and Neruda were poets, artists who made raids on the unspeakable. And in every poet, in every artist, there dwells atheist and ascetic, both libertine and monk, both Narcissus and Goldmund. Every artist (and this includes the musician) is simultaneously a hidden hermit and a political subversive, an anonymous ascetic and a howling philanderer.

This dual identity of the artist was eloquently described by Pablo Neruda some years before his death in a short essay entitled "Toward an Impure Poetry." Poets, Neruda insisted, are simply people who succumb to the curious attractiveness of the earth, people who see clearly the "confused impurity of the human condition," people who celebrate "the abiding presence of the human." Here is how Neruda expressed himself.

> It is well, at certain hours of the day and night, to look closely at the world of objects at rest. Wheels that have crossed long, dusty distances with their mineral and vegetable burdens, sacks from the coalbins, barrels and baskets . . . From them flow the contacts of man with the earth, like a text for all harrassed lyricists . . . In them one sees the confused impurity of the human condition, the massing of things, the use and disuse of substances, footprints and fingerprints, the abiding presence of the human engulfing all artifacts, inside and out.

> Let that be the poetry we search for: worn with the hand's obligations . . . steeped in sweat and in smoke, smelling of lilies and urine . . .

> A poetry impure as the clothing we wear, or our bodies, soupstained, soiled with our shameful behavior, our wrinkles and vigils and dreams . . .

One cannot be an artist, Neruda declares, without loving the impure poetry of earth: the meat and eggs and seeds that create our glory and our messiness. The abiding presence, the confused impurity of the human condition: love for this is what makes the artist crazy and gifted and godlike.

An artist is free, like God, to embrace the whole creation: its sweat and smoke, its lilies and urine, its perfection and impurity. But artists also know that imagination's liberty is purchased at the price of an exacting discipline. Art is, in fact, the supreme asceticism—and every artist's vocation includes a pilgrimage to the desert, a season of solitude, an eremitical toughness that shrinks the stomach and sharpens the vision. For the artist, Lent is a perpetual season; it is the inhabited universe of creative people.

Permit me to give some examples of this artistic asceticism. There is an old Jewish story that says God created the world not by filling up dead space with objects and things—but by *withdrawing* from space so that life in all its incredible variety could emerge and reveal itself. To put it another way, God "fasted" from space, *drew back*, so that the earthly beauty of plants and animals could shine in a human, habitable world. God creates by *fasting*; God creates by making self small so that *other* can live.

What this story says about God's own chosen asceticism could also be said about human artists. I think, for example, of the sculptor who stands before a block of stone and asks *not* "What can I make with this?" but rather "How can I let the form and beauty already present in this stone emerge and reveal itself?" Like God, the sculptor fasts: he or she is not interested in "filling up space" but in chiseling away the debris so that the life already present in stone can reveal itself.

Poets provide another example of this supremely ascetic discipline of art. We often think of poets as people who use lots of words—but in fact, just the opposite is true. The poet *fasts* from language, just as the sculptor fasts from stone and God from space. It is the poet's task to make a clearing in language, to cut down the undergrowth of careless, inattentive speech so that the deeper world of human experiences can reveal itself new, naked, fresh, and different. Poets approach language not as self-conscious masters but as self-effacing ascetics. Listen for a moment to this short poem by Robert Frost and you will see what I mean:

> Nature's first green is gold,
> Her hardest hue to hold
> Her early leaf's a flower;
> But only so an hour.
> Then leaf subsides to leaf.
> So Eden sank to grief,
> So dawn goes down to day.
> Nothing gold can stay.

The experience Frost describes in this poem is altogether ordinary; we've all seen and felt what the poet sees and feels: the first green growth of spring doesn't last; leaves fall and are replaced by others; dawn gives way to day—and Eden, that primordial symbol of human happiness and harmony, sinks down into grief and misery. Frost is telling us, of course, about impermanence and loss—about the loss in nature and about the more bitter loss of innocence. But notice that Frost tells us these things not by piling up words and explanations (as I have just down)—but by fasting from language, by choosing only a few lean words, none of them more than two syllables long.

Every artist is, then, both hedonist and monk, a voluptuous epicure and a contemplative ascetic. Music is surely a supreme example of the artist's dual identity. We create music not by saturating an environment with sound—which would be Muzak, not music—but by *fasting from noise* so that new sounds, new arrangements of pitch and rhythm and color, can emerge and be heard for the first time, as though we were present at the creation. We create music as much by creating silence as by creating sound. It is this controlled alteration of sound and silence that distinguishes *music* from mere acoustic pollution. Bach's "end-lessly rising canon"—the opening example—is a spectacular example of musical asceticism at its finest. Working with nothing more than eight measures of a fugue subject in the key of C minor, Bach creates a musical metaphor of infinity; he pushes our imaginations to the brink and puts us face-to-face with the infinite possibility of God.

"Hospitality"

The second element of a spirituality for artists is "hospitality." "Hospitality" is the art of creating a habitable environment for human beings. It has been said that the ultimate purpose of art is to render the "highest justice to the visible universe" (Flannery O'Connor), to create a world that human beings can inhabit. Whatever the medium may be—the language of poets, the brick and glass of architects, the stone of sculptors, the sound and silence of musicians—art seeks to create living space, breathing space for human inhabitants. And art that serves the Christian community is no exception: it too creates environments for people, not monuments for God. God, the prophet Nathan told David, doesn't need a house—and wouldn't live in one even if David built it. God goes where the people go, because God too is a pilgrim, a wanderer.

But this pilgrim God is also a host (or hostess), one who creates human space by setting a table for the hungry. And the proof of this is to be found at the beginning and end of the Bible. Has it ever struck you that the Bible begins and ends with food? The story of humanity's tumultuous relationship with God begins with food in the garden of Genesis and ends with the Supper of the Lamb in the Apocalypse. Eating got us into trouble in the first place—and eating will save us in the end (a wholesome thought that ought to bring mighty consolation to dieters!). In both Genesis and Apocalypse, God is a culinary artist, a host, a table companion. Where God is, there is food. And by the same token, humanity's "original sin" was nothing more or less than a refusal of God's hospitality: God threw a party and we decided to brown-bag it instead.

God's culinary artistry, God's hospitality, is an archetypal symbol of what every artist intends to do for human beings. Artists, too, feed and nurture the world. But there is more. A work of art is not only nourishment, it is also a symbol of the future—of that "happier order of things" when God and humans will again be table companions. Ultimately, art points to a reconciled universe, to a world healed and restored, to a human environment redeemed from ugliness. And this is true even when the artist's own life suffers painful diminishment, even when the artist is convinced that the "happier order" promised by God cannot be found in the world.

The following are a couple of examples of what I mean by artistic "hospitality." The first example is drawn from the art of poetry, while the second is drawn from music.

Nelly Sachs was a German Jewess who managed to escape to Sweden during Hitler's "final solution" of the "Jewish problem." Confronted with the unspeakable horror of the Holocaust, Mrs. Sachs found that she had nothing recognizably human left—except the power of language. Mrs. Sachs' poetry is an anguished chronicle of human destruction, written for survivors who know that in a genocidal nightmare no one really survives. Her poetry does not raise the dead back to life—but it does raise a solitary human voice in a world no longer human or habitable. Here is Nelly Sachs' poem entitled "O the Chimneys":

O the chimneys
On the ingeniously devised habitations of death
When Israel's body drifted as smoke
Through the air—
Was welcomed by a star, a chimney sweep,
A star that turned black
Or was it a ray of sun?

O the chimneys!
Freedomway for Jeremiah and Job's dust—
Who devised you and laid stone upon stone
The road for refugees of smoke?

O the habitations of death
Invitingly appointed
For the host who used to be the guest—
O you fingers
Laying the threshold
Like a knife between life and death—

O you chimneys,
O you fingers
And Israel's body as smoke through the air!

It isn't possible to comment on a poem like this one. We can only listen to it and hear a woman creating human space for unimaginable grief. And in that lies Nelly Sachs' act of artistic hospitality: she gives us space to mourn; she opens the mouth of a wound that lets us hear numerous human voices weeping in the nightmare.

My second example of artistic hospitality is a more familiar musical one. We all know the facts of Beethoven's biography: his unhappy childhood with an alcoholic father; his disappointing love-life; his miserable relationship with his brother and nephew; his descent into deafness. Beethoven's life is a Freudian nightmare, a textbook example of damaging psychological traumas. We know too that Beethoven's final symphonic creation—the monumental Ninth Symphony—was written when the composer was, for all practical purposes, stone deaf. And yet this final symphonic statement concludes with a triumphant "hymn to joy." Beethoven's final "assessment" of the world—a world that had brought him incredible grief and excruciating physical deformity—was a mind-boggling hymn of praise. As an artist, Beethoven reacted to a life that had brought him overwhelming misery by creating a habitable world of sound in which all of us can live. His ultimate symphonic testament was a supreme act of nurturing hospitality. Faced with his own death and deafness, Beethoven set a musical table at which all of us have feasted ever since. His hospitality was no accident; Beethoven knew what he was doing—and said so, in his Heiligenstadt Testament, written in 1802. Let me quote it, briefly:

> For me there can be no relaxation in human society . . . I must be entirely alone, and except when the utmost necessity takes me to the threshold of society, I must live like an outcast . . . Sometimes I have been driven by my desire to seek the company of other human beings, but what humiliation when someone, standing beside me, heard a flute from afar off while I heard nothing . . . Such experiences have brought me close to despair, and I came near to ending my own life—only my art held me back, as it seemed impossible to leave this world until I have produced everything I feel it has granted me to achieve . . . It has not been easy, and more difficult for an artist than for anyone else. O God, you look down on my inner soul, and I know that it is filled with love of humanity and the desire to do good . . .

Through his music Beethoven became the consummate host, spreading a feast and creating a human environment where all of us can find happiness and strength. Despite his painful life—or perhaps *because* of it—Beethoven's music became a sacrament of that "more cheerful order of things," of a world renewed and reconciled.

Respect for Symbols

These reflections on "artistic hospitality" lead to a third quality of spirituality for artists and designers: respect for symbols. Traditionally, Roman Catholics have thought of themselves as a community where symbolism enjoys supreme attention and reverence. As a matter of fact, however, Catholics are increasingly inept at identifying what symbols are and how they "work." Perhaps it's because in common English usage "the symbolic" is opposed to "the real"—as though contact with the one eliminates contact with the other. Perhaps, too, it's because symbols are all too often regarded as "objects," "pictures," or "things" that "represent something else" and thus have no independent life of their own.

First of all, let me say that symbols are neither objects nor things—nor are they primarily "representational." Symbols are actions, transactions; they are verbs, not nouns. In other words, symbols are generative; they create clash, tension, and movement. In language, for example, metaphor leads toward symbol precisely because metaphor generates clash and tension by putting two things together that appear not to belong together. Encountering a good metaphor is like accidently sitting on a porcupine: the event generates movement—and if it doesn't, there's something wrong with you or with the porcupine. Metaphor thus creates motion in language—and when that motion is regularly re-activated (in the context, say, of a single poem or of a poet's work), a "linguistic symbol" is what happens. The "movement in the rose garden," the "moment in and out of time" is, for instance, T.S. Eliot's generative symbol for the experience of transcendence in a world inescapably bound to history.

Christians have traditionally believed that the human encounter with God occurs within symbolic media—and that those media are active, fleshly, historical, and even "worldly." This is why the central symbol of Christians is a human being: Jesus of Nazareth, whose flesh and history are to be taken seriously. Jesus is understood to "symbolize" the ultimate transaction between God and the world precisely *because* of his humanity—not in spite of it. This is why Christians have classically resisted any doctrine that denies or denigrates the true humanity of the Lord. In a word, Jesus reveals "God-ness" in our world precisely in and through the transactions of human flesh—and because of that, Jesus is the ultimate symbol—the "sacrament"—of the meeting with God. Jesus *is* a symbol *simply by being himself*—simply by being a man who lives, works, eats, drinks, listens, heals, blesses, loves, and dies.

And this is in fact true of all symbols: symbols "work" simply by being themselves. If one has to "make" the symbol "mean something," then what one has is a mistake, not a symbol. All Christian spirituality appeals to the ambiguous power of symbols, but the spirituality of artists and musicians relies on them to a preeminent degree. Perhaps this point is nowhere more fully evident than in architecture. Along with the culinary crafts of cooking and meal-making, architecture is an aboriginal art: it carries us closest to our human origins. Archaic humans not only sought food and made meals, they also sought shelter and made dwellings. And we've been doing it ever since. I suspect that the reason for this is to be found in the inherently symbolic character of the human body itself. Our bodies are perceived not merely as tools, objects, or instruments, but as dwellings, as habitations. As such, the body is the prime symbol of human interdependence, of the need for dwelling together, of the need to share habitation as food is shared in a meal. In a very profound sense, meals and dwellings make us human—and in fact they became the premiere evolutionary characteristics that distinguished us from our closest primate cousins, the baboons and the chimpanzees.

Architecture inevitably confronts us with the ancient symbols of the body, the body-personal and the body-corporate. Perhaps this is why architecture exerts such an enormous psychological impact on human inhabitants. Bodies and buildings are woven together in a dance as ancient as our origins. Christianity recognized this fact in its ancient rites for the consecration of a church. In effect, the building was treated as a body: it was washed, anointed, fed, and clothed. These rites, as exotic as they are, were not mere Gallican distortions of Christian piety; they were in fact an acknowledgment of the ancient anthropological connection between human body and human building. They were also a frank psychological recognition that buildings have skins, organs, wombs, and faces. The image of the church as mother is not only theological; it is also—and perhaps more profoundly—psychological.

The archaic symbolic connection between human bodies and human buildings is especially evident in the Cistercian architecture of the twelfth century. The abbey church at Le Thoronet in southern France was built about 1135 A.D. and eloquently represents what St. Bernard liked to call "geometry at the service of prayer." Like most Cistercian churches, the one at Le Thoronet uses familiar architectural devices aimed at simplicity of style: a drastic reduction of visual stimuli and the use of perfect geometrical proportions. The result, of course, is a kind of contemplative elegance: quiet, straightforward, unadorned. The stones speak simply as stone—as stone interacting with stone, as stone interacting with light. And of course that sort of architectural statement was entirely congruent with the Cistercian ideology of contemplative peace and freedom from distracting stimuli.

But the curious thing about the church at Le Thoronet is its acoustics. Visually, the stimuli are drastically reduced: there are no paintings on the walls, no carvings on the capitals of pillars, no gargoyles on the choir stalls, no mosaics, and nothing but natural colors. But acoustically, if I may switch metaphors in mid-stream, the church at Le Thoronet is a horse of a different color. The building is so sensitive to sound that a pin dropped in the nave produces a full set of harmonic overtones and can be heard in the apse about thirty yards away. The geometric proportions of the church were such that the sound of singing voices in the space would give your body an "acoustical rub-down." The monks who sang the divine office in that building were actually massaged by sound, their bodies were responding actively (though unconsciously) to constant subtle sonic stimuli. No wonder those monks liked to go to choir—they were being massaged by the sounds and spaces of the building itself.

At the church of Le Thoronet, visual austerity was more than adequately compensated by acoustic sensuality. Body and building melded into a single symbol of the human church at prayer. While the monks chanted, the building massaged them; single-minded austerity joined the impure poetry of earth to create a symbol of the church, earthly and unearthly. And like all good symbols, this one spoke for itself, and required neither explanation nor apology.

In the final analysis, perhaps it is just this combination of austerity and sensuality—of asceticism and impure poetry—that marks the spirituality of the Christian artist and musician. Like the crazy gifted God of Jesus Christ, such a person joins the familiar human with the unfamiliar "other," the ascetic with the hedonist, Narcissus with Goldmund. Like God, the Christian artist is a contemplative with dirt under the fingernails, someone who simultaneously casts shadows and gives off light. Perhaps the great modern architect Louis Kahn said it best when he wrote:

Silence—the unmeasurable, desire to be, desire to express, the source of new need—meets Light—the measurable, giver of all presence, the measure of things already made—at a threshold which is inspiration, the sanctuary of art, the Treasury of Shadow. I said that all material in nature—the mountains and the streams and the air and we—are made of light which has been spent, and this crumpled mass called material casts a shadow, and the shadow belongs to the Light.

Shadows and light, asceticism and impure poetry, hospitality and respect for symbols: these are the elements of a spirituality for artistic people in the church.

* * * *

Now a few short implications for the ministry of musicians. The musician called to minister in the church is a *prophet*, not a caretaker. By this I mean that the musician challenges us with new ways to explore old mysteries. It is the musician's task to stretch the human imagination about God, to invite us to think about God with our bodies, our skins and our ears, and not merely with our intellects.

The musician exercises a ministry of artistic *hospitality* in the church. The musician's goal is to create a human, habitable world—an acoustic environment in which the mystery of God can be explored.

Musicians who serve the prayer and celebration of the Christian community do not have to assume another identity in order to be ministers. In other words, musicians are ministers *because* they are artists—not in spite of it. Musicians do not have to become "somebody else" in order to legitimate their ministry; their service *is* their art; their ministry *is* their music.

The minister of music is a *mystagogue*, someone who initiates others into mystery, someone who guides the community in its search for beauty ever ancient and ever new.

TWO

LAY MINISTRY AND LAY MUSICIANS

The encounter with music that I have experienced this year is somewhat unique. In January my eighty-five year old mother fell and broke her hip. For the operation to mend the fracture, she was given a spinal. During the operation she said to the surgeon, "When I feel low, I like to sing. Do you mind if I sing?" So, accompanied by a chorus of nurses, singing "I Love You Truly" to the surgeon, my mother turned fear into hope. In the hospital, while recuperating, using a wheelchair, she visited other patients. If they seemed "low," she often sang to them her favorite song, "I Love You Truly." Now she daily participates in the activities at an adult day care center where she encourages other elderly folk to sing along with her "I Love You Truly." About this she says, "None of us feel so lonesome when we sing together." What my mother has done with one song has helped me to perceive the healing, pastoral, and communal powers of music.

The effective ministry of music makers implies a recognition of these powers and the ability to utilize them in a way that invites the people to feel at home with God and invites God to work within the hearts, minds, and spirits of the people. My intention here is to share with you some insights an outsider has discovered about the ministry of music. My presentation is in four parts, which I refer to as genres.

LAY MINISTRY: THE POST-CONCILIAR CHRUCH

Community building, healing, evangelizing, offering hospitality, as well as, of course, preparing for liturgical community
gatherings—these are the numerous *commonalities* that should
bond the lay minister of music with other lay ministers. What I
find intriguing is the persistence with which the ministers of
music are perceived as somehow *not* cut out of the same cloth.

Sometimes the laity more than other lay ministers appreciate
the ministry of the music maker. In other words, many lay *ministers* still think that lectors and catechists, communion distribu-
tors and hospital visitors, lay pastoral associates, parish council
members, and social justice activists are the farmers and the foot
soldiers doing the basic, essential ministerial tasks on the good
solid green earth, while the music makers are pilots putting on a
fancy air show, providing a welcome respite or distraction from
the real doing that needs to be done. But if you *eliminate* the music
ministry, which may seem peripheral or taken for granted in a
parish, you'll rouse a hue and cry. Substitutes can sometimes be
found for other lay ministers. But because the music ministry is
characterized by very specialized natural talents, often nurtured
by a particular kind of education, the ministry itself, as James
Breig points out in *U.S. Catholic*, may attract mixed feelings—
envy, gratitude, resentment—that other lay ministries do not
evoke.

The music maker needs to either learn to live with this ambig-
uity of affectivity about his or her ministry or to come closer to
colleagues in other ministries and share stories. We are sometimes deceived. Your ministry looks like such fun; we forget what
hard and exhausting work it is.

Besides talking with colleagues and companions in ministry,
all of us who minister in the United States need to take a long,
loving, contemplative look at the setting for our ministry—post-
conciliar church life in the United States. If we tend to focus
instead on other topics or issues, it might be because looking at
the sweep of post-conciliar church life is like attending an opera,
having never read the libretto and not having an understanding
of the language through which it is being performed.

Contemplating the grand sweep of American church life is a
maze of diversities that evokes confusion. It is dangerous to

generalize about this vista. It is futile to propose one path through the maze or to fix blame for the existence of the maze in an absolutist way.

To say that *horizontal dynamism* has erupted in the church in the United States is about as far as I am willing to go in being declarative about the post-conciliar American church. (Bishop Pilarczyk describes this dynamism cogently in a letter to the Curia published in the 25 May, 1985 issue of *America*, crediting it to the nature of North American culture and society.) Of course, I have to add to my declarative sentence that some lay folk have never felt that dynamism because, in their parish or diocese, the hierarchical dynamism of the *preconciliar* church continues to prevail. And what many of us have experienced and are experiencing is the clash of horizontal and hierarchical dynamisms in our parish and diocese.

But, from my experience as a lay advisor to the NCCB's Bishops' Committee on the Laity, I can also say that it is fruitful to *explore* the territory that is the American church experience today and to inquire about commonalities that might be emerging. The Notre Dame Study of Catholic Parish Life, an interdisciplinary research project running from 1981 to 1988, is doing just that. Using thirty-six representative parishes, the Phase II part of the project is an in-depth study that "yields sufficient cases to generalize about each of the 36 parishes with a high degree of accuracy . . . And, through weighting procedures . . . generates accurate and valid findings for all non-Hispanic Catholics in the United States *within their parishes*" (*Notre Dame Study of Catholic Parish Life*, "The U.S. Parish Twenty Years After Vatican II: An Introduction to the Study"; (Report 1) ed., David C. Leege and Joseph Gremillion, Dec. 1984, p. 3).

Let me share with you some of the findings discovered in Phase II described in Report 1: "The first and most striking feature is that unpaid lay persons conduct many of the important ministries of the parish . . . The results show that beyond the parish priest, 83% of the leadership within Catholic parishes, paid or unpaid, are laypersons. Even among paid staff with responsibilities for key programs, 57% are lay . . ." Increasingly, leadership in the grassroots church is becoming lay.

The editors go on to say: "But lay responsibility does not necessarily bring with it policy control . . . The Phase II data suggest that while shared responsibility symbolized in parish councils is important, effective decision-making is either more centralized—in the pastor—or decentralized to the level of those laypersons and staff especially interested in a particular type of ministry or program."

According to the editors of Report 1: "The second striking feature about lay participation is that so many do participate and they do so in a wide variety of liturgically and religiously significant ways." Almost half participate in one or more parish activities beyond Mass: but only ten percent are visible in liturgical ministries, three percent as choir members.

The affirmation of music as a participatory dynamic within liturgy is *overwhelmingly* affirmed by the laity—a whopping ninety-four percent are pleased with the hymn-singing; only thirty-four percent feel the music generally needs to be improved, with only forty percent citing singing as most in need of improvement.

These statistics provide enough fabric for us to locate some strands with which to find our way out of the maze to a plateau where signposts will be clear enough for us to know what the emergent issues regarding lay ministry will be in the decades to come. Let me list those I perceive as vital.

1. Who will govern? Pastor? Professionals? Populist Consensus? The decades to come will surely bring more discernment, but perhaps also more struggle, about whether decisions and policies will be made primarily by pastors, or primarily by populist consensus, or primarily by professionals with specific ministerial responsibilities, or collaboratively by all three.

2. Voluntary Ministers and Professional Ministers—Allies or Enemies? When the Notre Dame Study looked at those lay readers who minister voluntarily, the evidence revealed that twenty-two percent spend an average of five hours a month on parish activities, twenty-five percent average fifteen hours, and twelve percent spend almost all their discretionary time in voluntary ministry. Relationships between those contributing without compensation and those who are paid staff persons—involving the sensitive issues of setting criteria, establishing rights, discerning rewards—must be more adequately addressed in the coming decades.

3. Structures for Ministerial Positions—Grievance Processes, Salaries, Job Descriptions, Support Groups. Sometimes career ministers feel inhibited about publicly addressing their own needs because voluntary ministry is perceived as more salutary. The NCCB document *Called and Gifted*, the NCCB *Pastoral on the Economy*, and more progressive dioceses realize that the church community is enhanced when the needs of those professionally prepared for ministry receive respect and a response based on justice. And in the U.S., justice means due process, fair wages, voicing dissent, the right to lobby, inclusion of women and minorities.

4. Training and Formation—Basic and Specialized. Another emerging trend that will lend to the lay minister a dignity the ministry deserves is the developing affirmation of spiritual formation and some generalist theological studies, as well as specialized preparation for any particular lay ministry.

5. Identity—Spiritual and Pastoral. I once asked a priest whether he perceived himself to be a minister of the church for God or a minister of God in the church. The next time I saw him he said, "I'm amazed that I'd never asked myself that question before. For the past two weeks it's haunted me and I'm still not ready to give an answer.

Many issues pertinent to present-day ministry in the church hinge on this neglected question of spiritual and pastoral identity. How you minister, your attitudes toward those to whom and with whom you minister, your ambiance within your ministerial setting, depend largely on how you perceive your own spiritual and pastoral identity, how *you* answer the question: "Am I a minister of the church for God or a minister of God within the church?"

I recently heard two stories regarding pastoral identity that reveal the ramification of the choices that confront the music minister. Two acquaintances of mine, each a member of a choir for years, experienced the trauma of a death in the family. The first, when I met her, recounted vibrantly the consolation she received in concrete and continuing ways from the choir director and members during her bereavement. The other, when I met her, told me she had, after eight years of service, quit singing with the choir after Easter. "The director and I had a blow-up during the rehearsals for Holy Week. I suddenly felt so hurt and angry because the director never once had extended even a word of sympathy about the death in my family, and I voiced my resentment right out—plain and simple and straightforward." I asked what the choir director had said. "That the bereavement committee in the parish was supposed to take care of that sort of thing," was the reply.

Here we have two different models of pastoral identity set out by a minister of music, each tied to self-perception of spiritual identity. I hazard a guess that the first choir director perceives self as a minister of God within the church, modeled on the way Jesus ministered. The second choir director probably perceives self as a minister of the church for God, modeling ministry on a bureaucratic dynamic that mirrors the specialization characterized by our culture, and the juridical framework of our church.

I will return to the issue of spiritual identity, but let me first review where the signposts for the future point and urge action in regard to them. Governance; the relationship between voluntary ministry and career ministry; just structures for lay ministers; education—training and formation; the spiritual and pastoral identity of the lay minister. If music ministers, individually and corporately, opt for a peripheral position in the emerging parochial, diocesan, and national dialogue and discernment on these issues, they and the incomparable contribution music makes to the spiritual and pastoral life of the church may be left by the wayside. I urge you to join organizations like the National Association for Lay Ministry (NALM), and give your partisan efforts as a form of caregiving for your colleagues and for our church.

As we together try to move forward with the horizontal dynamism, yet direct its energizing force in ways that are fruit-bearing for the mission to which the whole church is called, we do this within the context of yet another, and even more overwhelming change, a change in vertical leadership. The term priestless parish is heard more and more in church circles. When we have solidly turned the corner of the twenty-first century, we may begin to hear warnings about the priestless diocese. This is sad. Data about the decline in vocations to the religious life and to priesthood only make more imperative a passionate effort to resolve in a collaborative way the five issues at the heart of developing a substantive ministerial foundation within the church that is lay in character in order to have a viable church life in our nation to hand down to our children and grandchildren.

The future *of* the church is the priority issues *for* the church today. And let it not be said that pastoral musicians fiddled while the viability, vitality, and even the very survival of our tradition was at stake.

The worst mistake that can be made—a difficulty in the permanent diaconate—is to become hybrids and forget our layness. As Cardinal Bernardin pointed out in a Pentecost 1985 pastoral letter on Ministry: "Ministry appears to have two essential dimensions, relational and functional . . . ministerial activity is ultimately directed toward establishing a life in communion with God and with one another, a way of life which manifests the Kingdom of God in our midst."

This relational dynamic of ministry is of particular significance in the leadership role of the director of music in relation to the assembly of people and their praise and worship of God. Lawrence Johnson tells us in *The Ministers of Music* (Pastoral Press, 1983): "The musical exclusion of the people from the Mass had in most areas been completed by the 11th or 12th century . . . [and] the assembly became a congregation of mute spectators." This musical genocide of most of the laity lasted for 700 years. This fact heightens, I hope, the lay leader's bond with the people today.

With this in mind, those of us who are lay ministers may want to remember and affirm that we were called to our ministries from the *midst* of the assembly. Each and every one of us who is a lay minister leads not over and against the community of the people, not over and above the people, but sent *from* them as *one* of them. Our giftedness bears fruit only through the people, only by an incarnational dynamic. They may break our hearts because they don't fulfill our dreams, yet they are our salvation, for the people are how we are judged—not only at the heavenly gates but today as God asks of every minister, clerical or lay, "Where are you with my people?" You don't want to say, "I have no patience for your people." Or to admit, "I used the power you gave me to parade in front of your people."

Fidelity to the Spirit's call in Vatican II for the full and active participation by all the people in the liturgy means that, for the priest and celebrant and for the music minister, collaboration with one another and with the people is constitutive of their roles as leaders of the assembly. Metaphorically speaking, the music director, in his or her ministerial role, models *for* the presider and other liturgical lay ministers. Through preaching and sacramental action, the priest hopes to facilitate an ambiance whereby the people are motivated to work with one another and others beyond the liturgy, in society, in harmony, self-giving, and sharing. The music director, by relating to the assembly, is called to encapsulate that harmony within the span of the liturgy. But who ministers to the music maker in order for the music maker to minister to the people?

TRAVELOGUES—A TALE OF COMMUNAL CREATIVITY: BEING ARTIST IS MINISTERING TO SELF

Now let me go the Berkshires in western Massachusetts. I invite you to let me minister to you. I invite you to come with me for a few moments in your imagination.

Spend two weeks in the Berkshires with me. Let yourself become absorbed in the music of Tanglewood. Come with me to the Mount for Shakespeare under the stars, travel with me to Becket for Ballet at Jacob's Pillow, to Williamstown to see a Tom Stoppard play, to Stockbridge to savor the collected homey works of Norman Rockwell and to stroll through the grounds and studio of Daniel Chester French, creator of the Lincoln Memorial.

Culturally, the Berkshires are a cup of blessing; sipping from that cup restores a sense of self as artist. If you come with me, you'll return to your home and your ministry not only restored in heart, mind, and spirit, but aware in a fresh, vibrant way of your own creativity and the creative potential of your people and colleagues.

The artistic dimension tells the tale of how *creative* the minister of music is. In most places, music makers are the *visible* artists within a local community—often the only visible artists the community has. There's a legitimation here that evokes responsibility. To slight one's artistic dimension not only allows ministry to become a burden, it may diminish the effectiveness of one's ministry and the local church community.

But let's look at it the other way—at how sustaining artistic vitality and affirming one's layness can *enhance* community, ministry, and mission.

Let me tell you about The Vineyard in the Berkshires and how it differs from most of the parishes I've seen. The creative arts and faith are at the heart of The Vineyard. Within the community of about thirty-five families there is a conviction that each man, woman, and child has some creative dimension waiting to be nourished and to bear the fruit of communal activity.

For example, The Vineyard Community originated the idea of having week-long summer creative arts and faith workshops. Limited to fifteen people, who came from all over the country, the workshops were designed to encourage artists from a particular discipline to try their hand—or voice—in other disciplines and discover how allied, not alien, the arts can be to one another. Resistance to risking this endeavor was strong but eventually singers were on stage as actors, and trumpet players tried dance. One painter wrote a poem that got published in an anthology of poetry. And a social activist from Appalachia made a large stained glass window. Illuminated at night, it greeted and reminded the men and women in the area of God.

Within the horizontal dynamism of The Vineyard Community, love and justice flourished. The talents that emerged from the people were never stultified by becoming overly churchified, which is a fear I have for the music ministry.

The stories are endless when we realize in a more heartfelt way that God's gift of creativity is not limited to a liturgical rendition, whether that be in visual art, drama, dance, or music.

What is needed for this to happen? The need is for a greater development of the perception among all the people of the church that creating with the people is the *ministry*; music or drama the *medium* for the ministry. (We see parallels to this in other ministries, i.e., preaching is a ministry, the Word is the medium preached, and not vice versa).

What would *creating* with the people look like in a parish? If I were a minister of music new to a particular parish, setting my agenda for the first year would run like this. In recreational and contemplative settings, I would try to get to know the people with a keen eye and ear for *their* gifts and *their* musical interests.

Through singalongs and/or talent festivals that included drama, dance, and visual art experience, through workshops with other ministries, I would let the *vitality* of music be felt afresh outside of liturgy, trusting that later this would bear fruit in liturgy. For example, helping people learn and harmonize with familiar music in fun settings can pave the way for the future. These sessions are in a way rehearsals of musical dynamics that ease the way to adequately sung liturgy. More importantly, the people learn to trust and love the director of music, which nourishes the desire to collaborate with him or her. What motivates the creativity in The Vineyard is the complete trust the people have in their lay leaders and priests and the trust the priests and lay leaders have in the people.

A PLAY REVIEW AND CAUTIONARY TALE: SIN IN MINISTRY AND CHURCH

I urge you to read the paperback publication of *Amadeus* (Signet). *Amadeus*—love of God—that play and film by Peter Shaffer spells out awesomely the spiritual tragedy that can become the narrative of a believer's life. Paradoxically, it is our fortune to have this imaginative tale that can teach us about the spiritual risks of ministry.

In Antonio Salieri we encounter Lucifer, Adam, Caiaphas, and Judas. For a moment let us trace his tragic spiritual journey. It starts, of course, with Salieri's perception of God; an old God "staring at the World with dealer's eyes . . . eyes [that] have made bargains, real and irreversible," a God chained to the marketplace of *quid pro quo*. Salieri's second spiritual error is to sell his gifts for fame using this God as his agent to whom he promises conventional good and pious behavior. Later, when Salieri realizes that Mozart has no guile and is wholly transparent to the creative power of music, the twin demons of pitying self and finding a scapegoat ensnare Salieri. He compares his emptiness to Adam's nakedness and blames God for giving him the desire to praise God; then, caught in his own self-indulgent melodrama, he blames God for making him mute and blames Mozart for the increasing rottenness Salieri felt within himself.

The spiritual deck with which Salieri plays is absolutes. Music is an absolute, an idol. Fame is an absolute, an idol. Mozart, when perceived by Salieri as the Incarnation of God, becomes an absolute, motivating Salieri to name God as enemy—the most spiritually devastating of absolutes. Congratulating himself for his cleverness, Salieri lets the lust of envy lead to using his own power over God to block God working in the world and, through that madness, to do in a despised rival.

How to accomplish his dreadful task? Starve out the God, he cries. In the play when he crushes Mozart, Salieri commits his last sin—an attempt at robbing Mozart of hope in God.

Shaffer's Salieri is the antithesis of what the minister is called to be, for he lets his gifts shape his being into a vessel of spiritual sins. At the end of the play he warns us that he lies in wait as The Patron Saint of Mediocritie to ensnare us, to trap us into moral mediocrity. He can do that in one or another easy step.

If I am being somber, it is for three reasons, each of them being tied to ministry.

To marry ministry with a public display of one's talents necessitates strong ego and self-confidence. A ministry in the arts necessitates asking oneself whether one chooses to follow Salieri or Jesus.

Second, lay ministry, because it is a newly discovered horizon in the world of the church, can feel intoxicating at times. Yet, in more ways than one, the lay minister can feel put down, unappreciated, and oppressed. When the former collaborates with the latter, defensiveness can lead to spiritual snares. To hold one's own, one feels one can never err and forgets that the keys to the kingdom are not meant to be small enough to fit in anyone's hip pocket or large enough to use as a club over others.

Lay ministry is becoming a powerful movement within the church. As its momentum intensifies, it can threaten in a way similar to Mozart threatening Salieri. As a retreatant who resisted having me as a retreat director put it: "If I as a vowed religious thought God could work through you, a lay director, I'd look differently at all the lay people. I might begin to believe God could be incarnated in them. How would my vocation be special then?" We must expect, indeed anticipate, resistance or rage as a response on occasion from those frightened that their vocations are undone if our vocations are transformed.

These are some of the reasons why the spirit of Jesus, not the spirit of Salieri, must be at the heart of lay ministry and why your particular fundamental question is not, "Do I love music?" but rather, "Do I love God and God's people *more* than I love music?" And there will be no question of that if, measure by measure, your ministry has as its heart creating *with* the people.

Your talents marry *their* talents. A reversal of the story in *Amadeus*—the nemesis of some music ministers is working with those *without* talent, motivation, and good will within the assembly whom the music minister is called to lead. *Amadeus* can still be instructive; as a story conceived by Peter Shaffer, it is akin to an operatic drama but the spiritual errors and sins in *Amadeus*are common enough, aren't they?

> Perceiving God in a distorted form
> Nourishing a desire for fame
> Bargaining by promising goodness of
>   behavior in return for favors
> Envy, self-pity, scapegoating (Who
>   among us is fully free of these?)
> Blaming God Blaming rivals or those perceived as
>   inferior in some way for our not
>   accomplishing our self-established ambitions.
> Making idols
> Perceiving God as the enemy
> Starving the people of God by robbing them
>   of their feeling of worth and their hope.

It is naive to deny that these spiritual errors, these sins, exist in the church today. They may not be as apparent individual to individual but they rush in whenever we allow factionalism to infect a parish, a diocese, organization, or the Body of Christ we call the church. Whenever we donate our God-given talents and our ambitions and our efforts to the cause of making music or our ministry or lay ministry an *idol*, an absolute, or to making priesthood or vowed religious life an idol or an absolute, or horizontal or hierarchical dynamics idols or absolutes, or traditionalism or contemporaneity absolutes, we have succumbed to the spirit of Salieri and forgotten the spirit of Jesus. We then become accomplices in dismembering the Body of Christ.

It may seem far-fetched to find analaogies between *Amadeus* and the context of church, the context of our ministries, but enough of us can witness to the numbing of hearts and spirits brought about by spiritual sins to affirm that telling the story of ministry and leaving out the story of sin is like telling the story of Jesus' life and leaving out the cross. And when we do that, we rob ourselves of the power in truth that comes with risen life.

ACCLAMATION

Whether we speak of liturgical season or the life of faith or ministry in the church or the New Testament, a gift of the Christian tradition is that the journey is one of darkness to light—or of noise to song as Eugene LaVerdiere once said. Because this is lived out in the midst of the reality of neighborhoods and families and front page news, we need, at times, to stop and reflect on the milestones of darkness and noise becoming light and song in ministry. In the music ministry since Vatican II surely we have seen and heard this.

I would like to remind you of four of the particular and unique gifts of music ministry to the life of the postconcilar church. I see these embodied in the folk-song ministry that became, in a way, big business through records and compositions.

1. Just as we were beginning to wonder at the wisdom of loosening our grip on Latin and the dynamic of bonding through a universal language, along came the *Glory and Praise* hymnals to show us that what we need can be achieved in more than one way. Catholic folks from Massachusetts, Catholic folks from Minnesota, can still get together and talk the same language through hymnals.

2. David O'Brien, American Catholic historian, sometimes reminds us that for Catholics, having a national consciousness of the church is hard to come by because we are divided into dioceses that traditionally look to Rome, not to one another. But today we can celebrate the fact that the ministry of folk-song music came closest to that rare accomplishment of having a ministry that spans all the states and dioceses.

3. What is remarkable about this ministry is that its music makers (who need to become more inclusive of women and all minorities) responded with sensitive felicity. These music makers facilitated the powers of music to let God work freely among

God's people—the pastoral power, the healing power, the communal power.

4. Lastly, among a people living in a culture growing fiercely impersonal, the music ministry provided a solace that was personal, and there's nothing wrong with that. Show me a church that is impersonal, and I'll show you a church that is aloof from God, for our God is a personal god. Each of us has our own story of how a song or refrain has touched us and lifted us up when we, like the woman in hemorrhage, were mute with pain and afraid to speak to the Lord. In a time of great pain for me in the church, the only thread between me and God was the song *Come to the Water*. Sometimes I couldn't even sing it, but if I heard it at liturgy, or on a record at a retreat house, or on my tiny tape recorder, that one phrase "Except for the Lord" would echo for the rest of the day or the week and keep me going. It was God's gift that allowed me to endure.

In our ministries, because our shoulders are so often at the wheels of everyday detail and seasonal crises, it sometimes takes outsiders to say, "Lift your eyes and look back—you've come a long way. Lift your eyes and dare to look ahead—you're further along than you think you are. You and your ministry are doing a terrific job in contributing to the life of the church. Thank you from the bottom of our hearts." And this is my message to all of you who are music makers.

Beatrice Fleo

THREE

COLLABORATIVE MINISTRY: DO WE WANT IT?

The subject of collaborative ministry is important for anyone actively involved in the church's ministries today. But before I delve into collaborative ministry, I must set an appropriate backdrop drawn from Music in Catholic Worship's focus on musical, liturgical, and pastoral judgments.

Music is our art form, and we are entrusted with it as craftspersons and caretakers. Our first and foremost responsibility is to be the best musicians we can be. Dr. Raymond Spraque says: "If you ever do the perfect performance, you ought to quit while you are ahead; you'll never match it again. I doubt that anyone will ever do the perfect performance." We can never say that we have arrived as musicians; there is always something new to learn or improve on.

One quickly learns, however, that unless it is coupled with liturgical knowledge and sensitivity, all the musical skill in the world will not stop us from deeply violating and destroying liturgies. If we don't love the liturgy and see music as the liturgy's servant, if we don't grow in a knowledge of liturgical principles deeply rooted in the history and theology of celebration, then we must find another arena for our musical skills. Our love for liturgy must equal our love for music; ongoing liturgical education has to be a priority for us.

The concept of collaborative ministry falls under the pastoral judgment involved in musical worship. If we are not moving toward collaborative ministry, all the musical and liturgical skills in the world will only become tools of power to oppress people, weaken faith, and blind us to the body of Christ, contrary to the mission of the church. I can illustrate this with the following personal testimony.

A few years back I received a brochure describing a symposium in Dickinson, Texas, on "Celebrating Gifts." The brochure was homemade; I had never heard of any of the presenters; and Dickinson was not on my top ten list of cities to visit . . . so I tossed the brochure in the waste basket. By the end of the day I had picked the brochure out of the basket, read it again, tossed it aside, and gone home. I wrestled with that brochure for a week; it was a time in my ministry when I was really burned out, disillusioned with the church, and very hurt by past experiences. I was in no frame of mind to expend the energy and enthusiasm it would take to participate in that symposius, but I did it anyway. The group was small, only fifteen to twenty people, mostly clergy and religious, with a few lay people. In the discussions most of them found me to be angry, withdrawn, and bitter about the circumstances of the laity in the church. I just thought I was experiencing a little burnout.

I returned home a little refreshed from having been away, but a little disappointed because the symposium didn't fix everything as I had expected it would. Much to my surprise, though, I found myself sharing my experience with the rest of the staff, going back to my notes, rereading them, studying them, reflecting on them, and discovering how really important and significant the concept of collaborative ministry was becoming for me. It has made a profound difference in my approach to ministry, and although I am no expert in this field, I want to share the concept with you, so you can decide its value for yourself. Much of what you read here is based on the work of Brother Laughlan Sofield, one of the presenters at that symposium in Dickinson. He has since coauthored, with Carroll Juliano, *Collaborative Ministry: Skills and Guidelines*.

In its simplest form, collaborative ministry implies working jointly with others for the sake of the mission. It involves celebrating the diversity of gifts and using people's gifts creatively for building up the kingdom. Collaboration is nothing more than the identification, release, and union of the gifts of all baptized persons. The basis for collaboration is the belief that every baptized person is gifted and called to ministry.

If we want collaborative ministry, we have to want to work together to carry out the church's mission. We must want to be recognized as well for our own giftedness, so that we will have the freedom to use our giftedness with others to build up the kingdom of Jesus Christ in the world. But if we sincerely want to work together, why do we have so much trouble doing it? Because movement toward shared leadership necessitates change on the part of the people involved. And whether we are willing to admit it or not, most of us resist change. We want to hold on to the familiar, the secure, who we think or know we are, and we spend a lot of time and a lot of energy avoiding change and its challenges.

ATTITUDES AND CHANGE

Our very resistance to change helps us see some obstacles to our move toward collaborative ministry.

Competitiveness

The first obstacle is competitiveness. Our world fosters, values, and rewards competitiveness. Competition is not bad; it stimulates us to explore new expression of creativity and to unfold new avenues of human potential and growth. Team competitions teach the importance of working well together by combining and using talents to reach a goal. Only when we become blinded to the gifts of others and interfere with their freedom to use their gifts has the balance been tipped from healthy to destructive competitiveness.

When overly competitive individuals are asked to participate collaboratively as adult Christians in ministry, problems develop from the different attitudes that people bring concerning competition and from our desire to use ministry as a way to maintain and build our self-esteem. When we get too wrapped up in success, instead of sharing in the effort to succeed, we have tipped the scales from healthy to unhealthy competition. If winning is all that matters, and if being number one makes us feel important, then collaboration has no root from which to grow. Unfortunately our self-esteem is too often wrapped up in what we do instead of who we are—an unhealthy form of competition—and too often we equate self-esteem with perfectionism, so that when things aren't perfect or we recognize our own imperfection, we have to do something to make up for the drop in our self-esteem. Low self-esteem is sometimes expressed as depression, cynicism, or in fight-or-flight reaction, in which we either become belligerent or give way completely. A classic way of building up one's self-esteem is to pull others down.

Destructive competitiveness occurs among groups as well as individuals, as when neighboring parishes will implement one another's programs in a kind of interparochial competition, even when the programs don't meet the needs of the community. Some liturgists will implement colleagues' practices, even though they know their community is not ready for them, just to appear in step with current trends. When a contemporary choir or folk group won't be in the same room with a "traditional" choir, let alone minister at liturgy with them, or when soloists begin to feel alienated by other members of the choir, the competition is unhealthy.

Examples abound. One involves a parish that scheduled a week-long mission to be presented by a renowned person with skills in human development. The nun who arranged the mission suggested that the staff could use the opportunity for some staff development. But clergy support was minimal, so few parishioners participated in the mission, and the staff met as a group with the visitor once, with the pastor arriving late from another appointment.

Another example concerns the director of two of the three choirs in a parish, who was also the full-time salaried staff person responsible for the entire music program. It appeared that most of the time, energy, and resources went to developing the choirs under the baton of the paid professional. The other choir, the folk or contemporary choir, was never directly impeded by the other director, but its members were never made to feel valued or appreciated for their contribution to the parish music program. In fact, only the choirs under the professional's baton were included in a parish record album.

Parochialism

The second obstacle to collaborative ministry is parochialism, which is characterized by a narrowness of thinking, for example, "my program" or "our parish."

Christians should be about evangelization, not maintenance. Parochialism is a clear contradiction to Christianity's goal. A by-product of parochialism is the development of a closed system, a destructive element. In a closed system all energy is directed to maintaining the system; there is no willingness to bring forth new life and creativity. Any situation—ministry, community, parish, or institution—that has developed into a closed system ceases to be life-giving for its members.

I remember that a member of our small ensemble (eleven people, a close group very committed to ministry) lost a parent. We decided to provide an evening meal for this member's large family every day for a week after the death, so that our friend would have one less worry to deal with. The parish was divided into neighborhood groups, and I received a phone call from the chairperson of the musician's group. Rather than expressing appreciation for our work or offering to help, the chairperson accused us of interfering with the neighborhood group's activities, and an ugly conversation followed. How sad that a sincere act of Christian love and charity met such a response!

Some religious are experiencing parochialism in their communities. As they promote a new vision of the community's task or a more integrated community experience, some of my friends are frustrated, often by those in the community's leadership, by opposition to modernization, updating, or any kind of change. How many religious communities are dying because of their closed system, the destructive element of parochialism?

Arrogance

Arrogance is the third obstacle preventing our move toward collaboration. Collaborative ministry is not likely to occur when we approach one another from a stance of superiority. Sofield states: "Arrogance blinds people to the gifts of others as it attempts to protect their own images and self-esteem . . . When people believe that they have all the answers, they see no reason to look for complementary talents and gifts in others."

This mechanism to protect one's self-esteem is probably the most difficult obstacle to overcome because it is so hidden and ingrained. Sometimes it's hard for us in leadership positions to remember that our gifts and abilities are not superior to other's gifts, only different. On the other hand, people who feel victimized by those in leadership positions sometimes take on a posture of arrogance, thinking they are better qualified than the designated leader.

We readily see arrogance in others, but it is very difficult to admit and perceive in ourselves. We can all recount stories of religious and clergy who have conveyed superiority and arrogance to lay people by presuming they have much to teach the laity, but little to learn. In reaction, of course, some lay people presume they are better qualified than the clergy and religious for some ministries because they are working and living "in the real world." Such forms of arrogance are based on role rather than gift.

We need honest feedback from those who can assist us in coming to a fuller knowledge of ourselves. Friends and loved ones can gently call us to task and help us overcome the obstacle of arrogance.

Burnout

Burnout is the fourth stumbling block to collaborative ministry, because those who experience it do not have the energy or interest to engage in collaboration. Jesuit psychiatrist James Gill identifies the following types of people as vulnerable to burnout in his article "Burnout: A Growing Threat to Ministry":

—those who work exclusively with distressed persons;

—those who work intensively with demanding people who feel entitled to assistance in solving their personal problems;

—those charged with responsibility for too many individuals;

—those who feel strongly motivated to work with people, but who are prevented from doing so by too many paperwork tasks;

—those who are perfectionists and thereby invite failure;

—those who cannot tolerate variety, novelty, or diversion in their work life;

—those who lack criteria for measuring the success of their undertakings, but who experience an intense need to know they are doing a good job.

Burnout is a gradual process; it does not happen overnight. The initial phase is marked by an almost excessive, exclusive commitment to work or ministry. The actual amount of work is not as much a factor as the attitudes that drive the person. Here are five such attitudes:

—a good minister has no needs;

—a good minister is always busy, yet always available;

—a good minister can be all things to all people at all times;

—a good minister knows that idle hands are the devil's workshop;

—a good minister has no time for or interest in developing relationships; ministry is enough to sustain a good minister.

Internalizing such a set of beliefs creates unrealistic expectations that lead to an absorption in ministry to the exclusion of other aspects of life. So in the first stage of burnout you have a one-dimensional person obsessively committed to ministry because of an inability to set limits.

People in the second stage of burnout appear to be constantly tired and speak enthusiastically about how tired they feel, as if their effectiveness were equal in some way to how tired they feel. They also begin to ask questions: What am I doing with my life? What difference am I making anyway? Is it really worth all the effort?

Wrestling with these questions leads to the third stage in which people withdraw from others and display disappointment in themselves and their ministry: depression sets in. They tend to become overly judgmental of situations and persons, and their behavior drives others away, creating isolation.

The fourth stage is characterized by terminal cynicism brought on by an erosion of self-esteem. Lowered self-esteem is equated with free-floating hostility. Friends, coworkers, and everyone around are treated as adversaries subject to constant condemnation. Any energy left is focused on survival.

Many of us, under the guise of "ministry," think we are doing holy and good stuff, but we are actually running around in a constant state of burnout. Think again about the attitudes in the initial stage of burnout.

A good minister has no needs. We don't need good salaries, three balanced meals a day, one day off each week, let alone holidays and weekends. We don't need to develop relationships and be loved by others. We don't need time in our day for a little play, prayer, and exercise.

A good minister is always busy yet always available. Is your office door more like a revolving door, with a constant flow of people who just want a minute of your time? Do you feel guilty when you ask the secretary to hold your calls for a few hours, so you can get some work done? Do you overbook your work week to reflect sixty or seventy hours of work, as opposed to the normal forty hours, because a good minister must say yes to every request?

A good minister can be all things to all people at all times. Are you the priest who celebrates a funeral at noon on Saturday, a fiftieth wedding anniversary at 3:00 P.M., the eucharist for Sunday at 5:30, and a wedding at 8:00, still expecting to meet the emotional, physical, and social needs of all those people before and after each event? Or are you the musician who has a board meeting at a parish across town at 9:30 A.M., a staff meeting at 2:30 P.M., meetings with wedding couples at 4:30, 5:30, and 6:30, and a two-hour choir rehearsal at 7:30, only to return to the office until 11:30 to make a dent in messages and paperwork?

A good minister knows that idle hands are the devil's workshop. How many pastoral musicians regularly, without fail, take off work one full day a week, doing absolutely nothing that is related to ministry?

A good minister has no time for or interest in developing relationships; ministry alone is enough to sustain a good minister. God forbid that the parish priest go out to lunch with the parish secretary. People would talk! "Why develop relationships with others? I'm only going to be here a few years, then I'll get moved. It's too painful moving on and saying good-by." "Time to develop relationships, are you kidding? I don't even have time to go to the bathroom!"

BEHAVIORS AND CHANGE

So far we have discussed attitudes that prevent us from moving toward collaborative ministry. Next we will look at behaviors that do the same.

Hostility

The first is hostility, but we have to distinguish between anger and hostility. Anger is an emotion, neither bad nor good, positive nor negative. "Feeling angry" is not sinful, nor does it interfere with collaboration. Anger is nothing more than a spontaneous reaction to some stimulus; it is traced to three causes: frustration, a blow to self-esteem, or a perceived injustice. Anger produces energy that can be used constructively to overcome the frustration, build up self-esteem, or overcome the injustice. Creative use of anger can build collaboration; only when feelings of anger are converted into hostility is there an obstacle to collaboration.

Hostility is a behavior that seeks out an obstacles for feelings of anger and treats others as the enemy. Hostility poses a major barrier to developing collaboration, because others are not perceived as potential allies, but as adversaries to be overcome. Every minister will experience frustration, blows to self-esteem, and injustice at times; we cannot escape feelings of anger. The challenge is to discover avenues for expressing anger constructively, rather than converting it into hostility that will ultimately destroy any collaborative efforts.

I remember a wedding rehearsal at which the guest presider was present with the pastor of the parish and the wedding party. The pastor conducted the rehearsal, and as it went on, the visitor was getting more and more angry, feeling that he should have been running the rehearsal, since he would be doing the ceremony. Eventually his anger turned into hostility; to everyone's surprise, he stormed from the church building, to be pursued by the groom and part of the wedding party, who pleaded with him to return.

Dealing with Conflict

The failure to deal with conflict is the second behavior that impedes collaborative ministry. How many times have you heard it said (or said it yourself) that people who work for the church should be and act differently from those working in the secular world? Have you ever heard of priests who live in the same house not speaking to one another? Have you ever heard of parish staffs that are not models of peace and tranquility?

Despite the model of a church sharing all things in one heart and mind in Acts 4:32, the Scriptures are filled with examples of real conflict. Disciples argue over who is most important; Paul is in conflict with members of the Jerusalem church over the Gentiles; Paul and Barnabas fight over whether Mark should accompany them. To pretend that conflict doesn't exist and to suppress conflict in a group results in apathy and tension, which preclude collaboration. If collaboration is to occur, conflict must be confronted and dealt with. "Peace at any price" is not the way to deal effectively with conflict, yet it is the most common stance of those in ministry. Failure to deal with conflict condemns people to a state of no collaboration.

A parishioner once had a serious problem with a major project I was developing in the music program. Without checking the facts, he found people sympathetic to his cause and wrote letters to the liturgy committee, the parish council, the priest, and the bishop. I was not able to talk directly to him until he caused enough commotion to force a meeting of all interested parties. Only then did I have an opportunity to explain the project, correct the wrong assumptions, and enter into dialogue with the people's concerns. The originator of the conflict, though present, never opened his mouth. Everyone seemed satisfied with the outcome, but after the meeting, the conflict originator moved his membership to another parish. To this day I do not know what the real issues were for him.

Dealing with Loss

A third behavior that blocks our move to collaborative ministry is a failure to deal with loss. The impact of a loss is one of the greatest causes of stress, and too much stress interferes with people's freedom to be with and for others.

All loss is experienced on two levels, real and symbolic. The feelings caused by a separation or loss are not only painful in themselves; they trigger memories and feelings of previous experiences of deep loss. Since we are sometimes unable to deal with pain when it occurs, our psyche stores part of it, leaving the grieving process unfinished. Any future experience of loss acts as a catalyst to release the unfinished business from the past. Each time we experience a loss, then, we are dealing with the feelings of many losses at once, some conscious and some unconscious. If we understand this process we can see why what seem like insignificant losses, at times, can trigger strong feelings.

The more intimately one's self-identity is linked with an organization, group, or church, the more intense the feelings of loss if that group is threatened in any way.

When we are unable to deal with our feeling of loss and deny our experience of present and past losses, we will be unable to move toward collaborative ministry. Because our energy is used to protect us from past loses and prevent future loses, we become individuals who avoid intimacy and maintain aloofness from others. The Scriptures talk often about Jesus' great compassion for his friends and followers. We know that compassion has to be at the heart of our ministry, yet if we are aloof and distant, how can we express compassion or collaborate in its expression?

Another factor is the high mobility rate of ministers. We need to pay more attention to this factor as it affects the sense of loss we feel and the way that affects our ministry.

I had been working in a parish for six years when the music program reached a plateau, and it became obvious that further development would require major renovations of the church building, particularly the music area. We met with the pastor and agreed on a six-year process of study, consultation, development, and implementation. Within a year of the process' beginning, the parish threw a festive party to celebrate the pastor's fiftieth birthday. He had recently lost his surviving parent; he had only one sister and very few relatives. In addition, a favorite pet had just died. Suddenly his support for the program turned to opposition, as he faced the loss of the church he had known and felt comfortable in—the changes for music uncovered the need for other changes, such as the removal of the altar rail and the relocation of the tabernacle—on top of the loss of his parents and his youth. The conflict that followed led to the organist and me resigning three years into the program. After our departure, and much to the pastor's credit, for this was another loss for him, since we had all been friends, he completed the project slowly and painfully. Then he left. Perhaps in the midst of all this he was also wrestling with whether the parish needed new life that he could not supply, and he did not want to face yet more major losses.

"Learned Helplessness"

"Learned helplessness" is a phrase that comes from Leonore Walkers (*The Battered Woman*). It is usually used to describe an attitude of victims of physical abuse, but it also reflects a form of behavior that stands in the way of collaboration.

Learned helplessness is an attitude toward life in which a person constantly feels victimized. Studies of victims of physical abuse tell us that the victims often feel they have no control over their lives, and nothing they can do is ever going to effect the changes they want, so they live in passivity and helplessness. Even when some successes do come, their lowered self-esteem dismisses the reality, and they continue to believe that they are helpless. People who operate out of this posture have often been the recipients of continual negative reinforcement, which usually brings a lack of confidence and little self-esteem. They cannot appreciate their unique resources and giftedness. It is hard for them, therefore, to take the initiative and effect change.

How many clergy and religious, in the guise of the vow of obedience, are disillusioned and depressed because they feel the system is preventing them from working in the areas where they feel their real gifts and talents lie? How many lay people, who have been ingrained since childhood with the concept that "the priest is always right, and whatever he says, goes," continue to allow themselves as adult Christians to deny the equality of ministry we all received in baptism? We often find ourselves in a posture of learned helplessness as a convenient way out of having to take the initiative or the responsibility by resigning ourselves to whatever the pastor says, because "Father knows best," after all, or "that's just the way it is." Is it not in fact, a grave injustice to put such a burden of responsibility on our priests?

Sharing Faith

The fifth behavioral obstacle to collaborative ministry is our failure to share faith. This means more than not saying prayers together. How can collaborative ministry take place if we don't take the time to share with each other our stories and experiences that help unpack who we are in faith, so that others can come to know God working in and through our lives in unique ways? It is hard to conceive of any ministry group discovering how to "build up the kingdom of God," if they don't share faith and prayer with one another. Two conditions are needed for groups to share faith easily. The first is a climate that assures safety in sharing, and the second is an expectation that sharing will take place.

In many workshops and talks with liturgical groups I have discovered that people really do want to share their faith with others; they want to tell their story. I quickly outline different options for this exchange, so that even if people have never shared in this way before, or if they are uncomfortable with it, they can still participate. One option is just to listen, but usually about ninety-eight percent of the participants share with others that event or circumstance that is uniquely theirs, and what wonderful, powerful stories they are!

Once I was invited to give a talk at a parish and discovered over dinner that the group had never been together before. As part of the conclusion of my talk we did a faith-sharing circle. One by one we told our stories, power, rich in faith, and beautiful in the telling. One woman shared the story of her son's struggle with and death from cancer and her discovery of God in that pain. Another woman told of her desire to have a family and raise children and of the death of four of her children shortly after birth. (She is now the mother of three living children and the grandmother of six.) I heard one participant tell another, "I've known that woman for ten years, and I never knew that about her." One interesting dynamic in the group concerned three young men in their early twenties. Clearly they had never heard adults speak so profoundly and intimately before, with occasional tears and tight throats. When these three told their stories, they had clearly been influenced by what had happened. They admitted their limited experience in the faith, yet their stories contributed a youthful wisdom and honesty that the older adults benefited from. Only time will tell the real fruits of that sharing for those people as they minister together.

Sexual Integration

Failure to integrate sexually is yet another obstacles to movement toward collaborative ministry. Working in the church brings people together in personal and intimate ways, and those who have a hard time appreciating and recognizing their own sexuality may find this especially threatening. Sexuality as a gift is part of the total person that should be acknowledged, appreciated, and accepted. Past attitudes toward sexuality lead many people in ministry to repress this aspect of their being. Our challenge is to discover ways of integrating and expressing sexuality in ways that foster our ability to minister.

A lack of sexual integration may be expressed in two ways. The first is fear. Some of us become fearful of working with anyone to whom we might become sexually attracted. Often we spend a great deal of energy surpressing or repressing normal feelings, thoughts, and desires—energy that could be better spent elsewhere. And a lack of sexual integration can cause people to become obsessed with the sexual feeling they have, again to the detriment of ministry.

The more closely we work regularly with one another and the move we move toward collaborative ministry, the more we will have to learn to deal more directly with each other concerning our sexual feelings. The need for assistance and education in this area will become more apparent as collaboration gradually begins to take root.

I think the most blatant example of the lack of sexual integration lies in the structure of the church. The female perspective doesn't exist in the hierarchy, leadership, and governing body of the church of which we are all a part. Isn't it wonderful to see dialogue beginning between bishops and women as the first draft of the pastoral on women asks critical questions and expresses women's concerns? As article eighteen of that draft suggests, the challenge is to "call the church to a profound interior renewal, to a radical conversion of mind and heart, and to proper action in keeping with the directives of Vatican II."

* * * *

As an educator I know that the goal of teaching is to inspire and motivate others to want to grow in the knowledge for which I have provided a seed. They have to take that seed, plant it, nurture it, and bring it to life. To bring this seed to life you have to look to your own experience. Recall the times you have felt like a victim of someone else's arrogance, of burnout, competitiveness, and the rest. How did it feel to be blocked in moving toward collaborative ministry? You also have to be honest with yourself about the time you blocked and victimized others in the same way. You know what it feels like because you have been on the victim's side yourself. You have known the injustice, and you know what is required for forgiveness and conversion in the truth.

We ministers have to learn how to let go of the baggage we carry around with us. We have got to stop blaming others for hurts received and rendered in the guise of "building up the kingdom," and we have got to move forward to make collaborative ministry a reality in our lives, so that future generations will look on us as people blessed by God, because they will see in us the flourishing of the Holy Spirit.

The stark challenge of collaborative ministry is that the question in this article's title is wrong. "We" can't want collaborative ministry. It doesn't and can't happen in the we; it can only begin to happen in the I. We have got to stop thinking, feeling, and saying, "If only Father would . . ." or "If only the parish council would . . ." or "If only my choir would . . ." Wishing that some other person, group, or institution would change is a false understanding of collaboration, but given the reality of a situation or another person, I can change. I can act differently. I can open the door to a more shared style of leadership.

The bottom line is that collaborative ministry goes nowhere unless I have the courage to work through the obstacles myself, unless I continue to grow, reflect, and develop the skills necessary for others who work with me and experience me to be drawn into a more collaborative effort. I am called to change; I am called to conversion; I am called to be Christ's presence in the world today. Collaborative ministry: do I want it? This is what I must continue to ask myself, and I must wrestle with all it implies; this is the question for which I will ultimately be accountable.

Cynthia Serjak, R.S.M.

FOUR

THE MUSICIAN: TRANSFORMED THROUGH EXCELLENCE

It is more than time for musicians, even pastoral musicians, to be comfortable with the call to be excellent. Excellence is less a state of being than a *way* of being. When one aspires to be excellent, one never totally "arrives," or at least one does not arrive finally, but rather reaches moments of excellence, clarity, and integrity, as expansion beyond oneself into God. And the rest of the time we work at sharpening our skills, looking for better ways to sing what has been sung thousands of times already, while we wait for the excellent opportunity.

I invite you to think of excellence as stretching. If you excel in something, you stretch yourself to be better at it. But it's never something you grasp permanently; rather, it slips away, out ahead of us somewhere, to call us to stretch even more, to expand into greater understandings of who we are as we expand into freer and more excellent music making.

WHY BE EXCELLENT?

A first question about excellence is directed to musicians: Why should the musician be concerned with being excellent? Why should a musician expand and stretch? I think that musicians grow because expansion is essential to art. The poet Rainer Maria Rilke writes:

The deep parts of my life pour onward,
as if the river shore were opening out.
It seems that things are more like me now,
that I can see farther into paintings.
I feel close to what language can't reach.
With my sense, as with birds, I climb
into the windy heaven, out of the oak,
and in the ponds, broken off from the sky
my feeling sinks, as if standing on fishes.[1]

All of us who have brought a choir to the most excellent performance of an anthem have been part of the expansive dynamic of art, the shores opening out, seeing father into texts and notes. The process of working with a piece of music expands us.

We begin with excitement; we see or hear the piece of music and are taken by it, caught by it. We examine it carefully, and even in that first flirtatious hearing it in our own head, we expand, because the music lures us into its own space and time, its own unique presentation of reality. It calls us to hear notes in a different way, in a different combination, to feel rhythm in a way we hadn't before. Already we've been changed.

The initial encounter may end here. Perhaps we think the music asks too much of us—we see ourselves expanding into hours of practice time that we don't have. We feel our fingers stretching into chord positions that they haven't learned before. We cringe to hear sopranos straining to execute the expansive melody line. Or we may judge that the music asks too little of us; it doesn't offer us an exciting space into which to move. Perhaps it offers no space at all because it is so one-dimensional: we *could* perform it, but it lacks the magic and power to transform us, the excellence to motivate us to stretch and grow.

In a 1988 issue of *Pastoral Music*, Aidan Kavanagh wrote that "the truly beautiful never constricts or shackles the human spirit but always frees and enables it."[2] The truly beautiful, that which is worthy to be called excellent, urges us to expand into it, to see further into a painting, to get into a relationship with it, to get mixed up in its life.

Music making does not work automatically (*ex opere operato*), however, but requires work and practice. So after our initial enticement, if we choose to continue our relationship with the music, we may spend hours with it learning its intricacies, patterns, and secrets. This part of the process can be dark and strenuous and groping, even exasperating. It calls for patient altertness and a trusting stubbornness that eventually we will come to know the music as the music leads and teaches us.

This part of the music-making process, getting beyond the moment of a falling in love, working hard to build a relationship between yourself and the music, is the most mystical part. While we are unaware of it, the music begins to work its magic on us, leading us into its own reality, stretching us into its space, even across centuries, to touch an ancient harmony or a long-dead composer. This mystical work is not easy; it can even exhaust you or turn your head inside-out. But if you stick with it, it will carry you into the excellent feeling of singing well, the balanced feeling of playing a Bach trio sonata, the integrated feeling of being at one with your instrument. You will be caught, and you will leave the practice time humming the tunes and tapping the rhythm. You will remember what it meant to be inside the harmony, and you will become a co-creator with the music.

So the musician is transformed from a not-knower to a knower, from someone unsure about love to someone deeply in love, from a bored believer to a dancing mystic. This exhilarating experience is of the same fabric as excellence. The musician is called to be excellent by the music itself, by the richness and depth of the art.

I have been using the words "stretch" and "expand" to describe what excellence asks of us, but excellence does not call us out of ourselves in a way that leaves ourselves behind, or in a way that we are used up, or lose our identity. The excellent runner, who excels at running, uses her body well, uses who and what she is, focuses it, stretches it, but always remains at home and alert to her body. The musician who works to be excellent stretches to better music making, but does not get lost in the process, does not lose control of one's skills or talent. Falling in love means expanding into the other's space, while still maintaining one's own identity. To do otherwise is to leave much of love's labor unexplored.

Novelist and journal writer May Sarton says:

At any age we grow by the enlarging of consciousness, by learning a new language, or a new art or craft. That implies a new way of looking at the universe. Love is one of the great enlargers of the person because it requires us to "take in" the stranger and to understand him, and to exercise restraint and tolerance as well as imagination to make the relationship work. If love includes passion, it is more explosive and dangerous and forces us to go deeper. Great art does the same thing . . .[3]

To expand on Ms Sarton's thoughts: Without passion, without the explosive and, in a sense, dangerous engagement with the music, one may well miss the potential for excellence.

Another image for this experience comes from the potter M.C. Richards, who describes her attempts at centering the clay on the potter's wheel in this way:

If I begin at the center, firmly and gently, and if I open my clay firmly and gently, pulling the walls out from the center, opening wider and wider, as wide as the clay will allow, this crescent will form within me like a grace.[4]

The musician is called to be excellent, to begin at the center, to open yourself firmly and gently, pulling the walls out from the center, opening wider and wider and wider, as wide as you will allow, so that a crescent forms in you like a grace. The musician is called to expand like clay in the potter's hands or like lovers in each other's arms.

THE CHURCH AND EXCELLENCE

But we are musicians who are pastoral, who work with "church." So in addition to asking why the musician needs to be excellent, we need to ask a second question: Why does the church need us to be excellent? Of the many possible answers, I want to focus on one. The church desperately needs musicians to be excellent because the single greatest conversion that still needs to be worked among us, despite all our efforts at liturgical renewal, is for all of us to move from watching to doing. And music has great potential for enabling this conversion to take happen, if its performance is enticing, if it stretches beyond the mediocre, if it invites us and urges us to see more and feel more and know more about who we are and what it means to be church. If the musicians have worked enough and dared enough to enter the space of the music—the sacred music—then the musicians are working with a great power. This is not the "power over" of patriarchy and force ("You *will* sing!"), but "power with," the enabling power of unlocking the flow of the most excellent, magical, musical, mystical song.

Take the gathering hymn as an example. I'm sure you know that the General Instruction of the Roman Missal lists four reasons for singing a hymn at the beginning of the rite.[5] First, we sing to *begin*; that's obvious, someone needs to get us started. Second, to *deepen the unity of the people*. That should send up a red flag: the word "deepen" presumes that there is already some unity, and if there isn't, you should stop right there and talk about it. The song *can* deepen unity that is already present, which people bring with them when they come, even if that unity seems to be struggling around bolted-down pews, sorting through morning sleepiness, or recovering a fragile dignity after surviving the parking lot. Music can deepen unity because it gets people breathing together. The church breathes together, and everyone's breath gets mixed up with everyone else's—*everyone* else's. What an exciting exchange! You can't say that won't transform a community, but it will take as many verses as it takes for things to be so exchanged that there is neither Jew nor Greek, slave nor free, male nor female. That's called the Mystical Body.

Third, we sing the gathering hymn to introduce the feast or season. The Mystical Body breathes in the smells of Advent, Christmas, and Epiphany, Lent, Easter, and Pentecost. The song invites the Body into that special liturgical space (I don't mean the building) of pain and anguish and loss, of joy and glory and freedom, of mysticism and mission. And that transforms them mightily.

The fourth reason for the song is to accompany the procession. The song is for the Body, all the Body, and it expects them all to enter it. The song will take as long as the Body needs to feel itself established once again as *this* local Body of the church. Some of us may be there for days! But can we dare to proceed to the word, if the assembly doesn't even know who it is?

So the community—the church—is transformed from unknown to known and knower, from dubious about love to well-loved and lover, from distracted to attentive, from disillusioned to trusting, from boredom to mission . . . if the musical prayer is excellent, if it stretches itself open so that the folks can get into it, if it stretches *them* to reach across space and time until Jesus comes again.

A second ritual moment for transformation through music is perhaps the best-kept secret of the Roman rite—the preface and its acclamation, "Holy, holy, holy." It calls us to expand the Mystical Body assembled in *this* church, on *this* day, in *this* region to be at one with the Mystical Body of all who celebrate with us. That includes humans of all shapes and colors as well as creatures whose songs answer their divine calling: "Holy, holy, holy, most holy God of power and might. Heaven and earth are full of you." This is a cosmic song, one that stretches us all the way to the ends of the universe, and there the song still echoes: "Hosanna! Hosanna!"

How can the music be excellent for this moment? How can it transform this extemporaneous gathering of folks into the cosmic ensemble that is called for? The document Music in Catholic Worship tells us that the acclamations should be shouts of joy, that the music should be so well known that it bursts out of us. So part of the excelling needed for this song is finding music that enables the assembly to enter the cosmic shout, to open their eyes to the glory of all creation, to move them from watching (in case they still were) to doing eucharist.

We haven't yet found the right music for this song, partly because we still consider it only a people song, and so we haven't been able to hear the cosmic tunes yet. There has been some good stretching in that direction, but then my opinion is that the "Holy, holy, holy" should always be danced by the assembly, so I'm still looking.

THE PLANET AND EXCELLENCE

Calling to mind the cosmic song of the "Holy" brings me to my third question: Why does the planet need us to be excellent? What does it mean to be a musician during this time in the planet's history, when forty thousand children die each day from hunger; when our rivers and skies are so polluted that, by the year 2000, one-fifth of the world's current plant and animal species will be extinct; when the planet's forests are being destroyed at the rate of four thousand square miles a year; when we have the capacity to destroy life on the planet many times over?

Not long ago I felt that I should stop being a musician and begin working directly to stop the madness of nuclear build-up and ecological destruction. But something in me hesitated, knowing that the musical gifts I have are very much a part of who I am. I wrestled with this question, and I turned to music to teach me what I have to offer the planet and the global civilization that inhabits it.

For our Native American sisters and brothers, the question to be asked every day is: What is my relationship to the universe, and how do I express that relationship? What will I do today that reveals and enhances my relationship to the universe, which has worked so hard to give birth to the human species? For us, even to ask these questions may be a problem, since we have not been in touch with our cosmic origins. Our western, technologically oriented minds have objectified the planet and the universe, and we tend to think of the earth, the sun, and the stars as "its."

Native Americans, our oldest sisters and brothers on this land, and cosmologists, scientists who study the universe and its life, who are our youngest sisters and brothers on this land, are helping us to wake up to the reality that the universe is not a thing, but a living being who has shared its life in a unique way with this planet. We have the only water yet found in the universe (of course, we can only look as far as our equipment will allow). Drought teaches us the value of water, and some of us find ourselves asking, for the first time, what it would mean to be without this precious gift, and what is my relationship to it? This is a more profound question for those of us who have been baptized in water.

Taking a cue from these brothers and sisters who are asking the big questions, we can look at how the universe is, to see if we can find our story in that big story. Since the first moments of creation, the universe has been expanding. Even early humans who watched the skies noticed that everything seems to be moving away from us, giving us the illusion that we are the center of the universe, as the Greeks thought. Perhaps we needed some time to think that way, just as a young child needs a certain grounding, a feeling of being the center of everything, to be able to risk growing and exploring the world.

Copernicus began to tell us that we are not the universe's center, or even the center of the solar system (and we condemned him for saying it), and later we heard that things seem to be moving away from us because everything is moving away from everything else as the universe expands. At first we couldn't listen; we didn't want to hear it. But now that we're older and wiser, we are able to open our eyes and horizons a little more. We can begin to let the reality of this expanding universe become part of what we know and relate to.

That expansion is echoed in our call to move out of a pre-occupation with nationalism and into global ways of thinking. We are not always ready or happy to do so, but current crises are forcing us to do so. From the centuries of building up national defense walls, we can now work to stretch over those walls to take the hands of many friends and learn who we are as a global community. As cosmologist Brian Swimme comments: Thank God the earth is round, so that, sooner or later, we would have to meet one another and work with one another to survive and live in peace.[6]

What does all this have to do with making music. I want to borrow now from some of my work in *Music and the Cosmic Dance*.[7] Two questions: What are some of the qualities one needs to make music? And are those qualities helpful in thinking about the situation in which we find ourselves as citizens of this planet?

Two very important qualities in the music-making process are honesty and humility. We should be honest about the talent we have been given for musical work, our strengths as well as weaknesses, and not be embarrassed by how good we are. At the same time honesty demands that we recognize our music-making skills as gifts from a creative God through the hands of all our music-making ancestors. So we also need to be humble (from the Latin *humus*, meaning "ground"). In humility—with our feet on the ground—we recognize that the power of music is not our invention and music's origins are a mystery. We know that we have received from the earth the strength of bone and muscle for shaping our music.

A third quality is the reverence with which we approach the music, respectful of the power that lies there to excite, even exhaust us, the power of a melody to inspire, touch, and haunt us, the energy of harmony to enfold or caress or shake us and turn us upside down. And so we touch the notes in reverence, for we are playing with fire, the musical fire of the universe, and we humbly ask to be a partner in this conflagration.

When we ask that, we learn that music making teaches us "power with," for we cannot coerce the music into revealing itself to us or injecting itself into our fingers. We need to dialogue with it, play with it (often hard work). How many of us, thinking that we know music, approach it arrogantly, then suddenly find that we don't know it as we thought when our fingers stumble or our voices waver? That's not the music's fault; it's ours for thinking that we had the music in our power. The mystery of music's power is "power with," playing with, inviting others in, learning something new each time we play or sing.

To make music with others, we must trust that they will do their part and not play too loudly, too fast, or without care, that they have come prepared and practiced. We must trust our own skill to develop with us as the music requires. We trust the composer that the music on the page is worth our time and energy. We need courage to try the new, play the unplayed and unheard, and risk entering the creative process.

These qualities, so obvious for musicians, are the same ones needed to move us into the global civilization, which is the first step in assuring the planet's future. In humility and honesty about who we are, we can risk letting go of violence, war, and being "number one," and learn the pleasure of living in harmony. As the music teaches us "power with," we can learn the excitement of sharing power with others, learning from them as well as teaching them. We can let go of domination and learn cooperation; we can let go of having too much and learn the delight of seeing everyone have enough. As we study the various cultures that enliven our planet, we need reverence to recognize the beauty in all those faces and languages; far from extinguishing them we should be celebrating their wonders. And we badly need trust to begin finding a way out of the violence that has us bound in fear and unable to risk loving those who are different from us.

All this requires discipline and practice; we cannot become a peaceful planet overnight. Who better than musicians to teach us? We all know that music needs time and patient work to get it going, and careful and sensitive practice is needed to make the music we hear in our hearts. The planetary community needs teachers who exemplify the trust, humility, patience, reverence, discipline, and courage that the planet needs to survive. Who better than musicians?

Psychologist Jean Houston says that "the ecological crisis is both external and internal, for it has to do not only with an overuse of our external environments, but also with a gross underuse of our internal environments."[8] Who better than artists to show the planet the importance of expanding from a disciplined and practiced heart into the music of the universe? As artists we must excel and be examples of living together in harmony; as musicians we know that harmony often involves dissonance, and we learn respect for dissonance. Living in harmony does not mean there won't be conflict and tension, but it does mean respect for different ideas and ways of living and the care that may weave these sometimes dissonant lines together in great mystery and awe. In his reflective book *Out of My Depths: A Swimmer in the Universe*, Paul West writes: "We are the heart of things, the spawners of ecstasy, and however emotional we are is how emotional the universe is. The music of the universe, at least the solar system's, begins and ends in our own hearts."[9]

What about God? Does God need us to be excellent, as we do, because the music requires it, the church badly needs it, and the planet counts on it for survival? God invites us to excel and expand because stretching into God is who we are—theologians call it "divinization." God stretched very far for us in calling the universe to life, stretching a hand into Egyptian bondage to yank us out, expanding into our very flesh in Jesus Christ. How can we not respond in stretching gratitude? Jesus invites us to share his flesh and blood until he comes again, and we stretch on tiptoe, we groan (Rom 8) looking for that day.

If we musicians are accused of being out on the edge, let's rejoice, for "out on the edge," as Kurt Vonnegut writes, "you see

all kinds of things you can't see from the center . . . Big un-
dreamed of things—the people on the edge see them first."[10] But
stretching into us, God remains who God is at the very center of
everything. We stretch from a humble grounded core and remain
who we are, attached to the folks in the pews as well as the ones
watching on the hills; we grow deeper into our roots as our hands
stretch to find the music yet unheard. And as we stretch, there is
more room inside us for music, church, the universe, and God.

Finally, once again, the words of Rainer Maria Rilke:

> I live my life in growing orbits
> which move out over the things of the world.
> Perhaps I can never achieve the last,
> but that will be my attempt.
> I am circling around God, around the ancient tower,
> and I have been circling for a thousand years,
> and I still don't know if I am a falcon, or a storm,
> or a great song.[11]

Notes

1. Rainer Maria Rilke, *Selected Poems of Rainer Maria Rilke*, trans.
Robert Bly (New York: Harper and Row, 1981) 101.

2. Aidan Kavanagh, "Eastern Lessons on Liturgical Music," *Pastoral
Music* 12:3 (February-March 1988) 68-69.

3. May Sarton, *Journal of a Solitude* (New York: W.W. Norton and Co.,
1973) 93.

4. M.C. Richards, *Centering* (Middletown, CT: Wesleyan University
Press, 1962, 1964) 98-99.

5. General Instruction of the Roman Missal, no. 25.

6. See Brian Swimme, "Round Roots, Rounded Roots," *Creation* 1:5
(November- December 1985) 16.

7. Cynthia Serjak, R.S.M., *Music and the Cosmic Dance* (Washington,
D.C.: The Pastoral Press, 1987).

8. Jean Houston, *Lifeforce: The Psycho-Historical Recovery of the Self*
(New York: Delacourte Press, 1980) 13.

9. Paul West, *Out of My Depths: A Swimmer in the Universe* (New York:
Doubleday Anchor, 1983) 26.

10. Kurt Vonnegut, *Player Piano* (New York: Delacourte Press, 1952)
73.

11. Rilke, *Selected Poems* 13.

THE PRACTICE

FIVE

THE MIND-SET OF
A MUSICAL MINISTER

My subject is the mind-set of a musical minister, and I am going to treat it in three parts. If I were to give a subtitle to this article, it would be "Sonata for Three Hands." First, I'd like to say something about the meaning of ministry, then something about its vertical and horizontal aspects. In my own mind-set as I offer you these reflections, I'm going to be thinking of priesthood as the prime analog of church ministry, because that's the ministry I'm most familiar with. And I'm going to be using as my frame of reference among pastoral musicians the parish director of music. I know that not everybody reading this is *the* parish musician, but I hope that much of what I have to offer will also apply to choir members, cantors, and instrumentalists.

MEANING OF MINISTRY

Let's begin by talking about the meaning of ministry. I think there is a lot of imprecision and confusion abroad today about the nature of ministry. As things have developed over the last couple of decades, the concept of ministry has undergone significant change. Some of us remember the time when the only ministry in the church seemed to be the ministry of the ordained priest. Father did it all, and nobody else did anything. Now we have reached a point where it seems that *everything* that *anybody* does in the context of Christian life is some form of ministry. I believe that this last state is worse than the first. Using the term "ministry" to describe everything and anything is inexact and eventually harmful. If everything is ministry, then nothing is really ministry.

I prefer to use a more precise concept. I look on ministry as that which comes about when a member of the church is called to serve the church in the name of the church. Members of the church do lots of things as a result of their membership in the people of God. They witness to Christ in their jobs, in their neighborhoods, in their homes. They offer loving service in countless ways to those around them. They pray for one another. All that is good, but not all this is ministry. What people do is not "ministry" until they are called by Christ or by a representative of the church to exercise some office for the church in the name of the church.

The determinant of ministry is the call. Because holy orders is a sacrament, the call to the ministry of bishop, priest, or deacon ultimately comes from Christ. The call to other ministries comes from representatives of the church. Church members can be doing wonderful things, but what they do, strictly speaking, is not church ministry until they do it at the behest of the church and in the name of the church.

Likewise, there is no such thing as a private ministry. If it is ecclesial ministry, it is public and it is under the direction of the church. There's a TV commercial that's relevant here. It shows the supervisor of inspectors in a factory that makes men's underwear. Her big line is: "They don't say Haines until I say they say Haines." It's not ministry until the church has called it forth and authorized it.

There are some implications of this for parish ministers of music. First, because we ministers serve in the name of the church, we are obliged to follow the will of the church. Bishops and priests are not free to preach whatever they choose. They are agents of the teaching church and must preach all and only that which the church teaches. Ministers of music are not free to do whatever they want with music, because as ministers they are agents of the church in the context of the church's liturgy. This means that you have to be very clear about the purpose of music in the liturgy. You have to know what the church has said about music in the liturgy. You have to be familiar with the teaching of Vatican II and with its implementing legislation as regards your ministry. I sometimes think that it would be a good thing for bishops and priests to sit down every year or so and carefully re-read the General Instruction on the eucharistic liturgy. We get so used to things that we can get sloppy without realizing it. It might be just as good for church musicians to read over with some regularity the documentation that applies to them.

The second implication of ministry is that ministers are called to perform a certain service for the church. But that doesn't mean that they are just functionaries, mindlessly carrying out their tasks. Today more than ever before, there is need for ministerial creativity, for finding new and exciting ways to do what needs to be done. We can't afford to get into a rut. The restraints and restrictions that go with every ministry are not modalities of suffocation but merely the limits that every living thing experiences, limits that assist it to grow in the right direction. The restrictions of eighteenth-century Lutheran liturgy don't seem to have stifled Bach. The church needs ordered activity.

The third implication. Just as priestly ordination alone is not a guarantee of effective priestly ministry, so also being a parish musician, having been called by the church to serve, is not of itself a guarantee of effective music. Skills are required, and practice, and leadership. Do you remember when guitars were first used in church? Pastors thought that having guitar music for Mass would bring the young people in. In many cases the guitarists weren't very good. In some cases they were very bad. The young people didn't come, and after a while lots of other people didn't come either. This episode still has lessons for us today. To try to minister without skill, or to ask people to minister without skill, is to take advantage of the church.

The fourth implication. Because ministers are called and deputed by the church, they have a right to know more or less precisely what's expected of them. Hence, it is proper, even necessary, to provide all ministers, including music ministers, with a clear and precise job description. They also have a right to appropriate remuneration.

So much for the meaning of ministry, and for the implications of being called by the church to use your talents for the good of the church and in the name of the church.

VERTICAL DIMENSION OF MINISTRY

Let's now turn to the vertical dimension of ministry and explore some of its many implications.

The minister acts in the name of the church and assists the church to carry out its mission. When all is said and done, the church's mission is the mission of holiness, of helping people to be in touch with God. Ultimately, therefore, all ministry is somehow concerned with putting or keeping people in touch with God. For this reason, every minister of the church must be a person of prayer.

As I refer to prayer, I am thinking of prayer in all its various forms: public prayer, private prayer, prayer of petition and praise and sorrow and thanksgiving, mental prayer and vocal prayer, and so on. I would add that prayer in its deepest manifestation is not so much an activity as a state of mind. Prayer has been defined as wasting time with God, and it has been a conviction of mine for a long time that unless we waste quite a bit of time with God, we're not going to achieve much in ministry.

The reason why ministers need to pray is because prayer keeps us aware of whom we're really working for. In priestly ministry, we can very easily get glib and superficial and self-satisfied if we don't pray. We can also get bored and discouraged if we don't pray. If we priests and bishops don't pray, we soon forget what we're there for and what is supposed to be ministry becomes merely a job. I suspect the same is true with ministers of music.

Let me now suggest some implications of this need for prayer in the life of the pastoral musician.

First, everyone who ministers in the name of the church needs a disciplined regimen of daily prayer. You know what happens to your musical skill if you don't practice your instrument every day. The same thing happens to your spirit if you don't pray every day.

Two. Consider praying with your collaborators, that is, with choir members, instrumentalists, other parish ministers, the pastor. It's a lot easier for everybody to stay aware of what they're doing and why they're doing it if they have consciously shared together the presence of the Lord.

Three. Keep aware that the actual carrying out of your ministry of music involves prayer. The basic function of music in the liturgy is to help people to pray. Don't overlook yourself among those being led toward prayer by your music. Let me offer a personal experience in this context. I spend quite a bit of time each week in church at confirmations, parish visitations, Masses for special groups, and the like. If I'm not careful, I find myself carrying out functions and overlooking the opportunity for personal prayer that those functions involve. For some reason, the easiest thing in the world to overlook is the obvious.

HORIZONTAL DIMENSION OF MINISTRY

Now we come to the horizontal dimension of ministry. Perhaps one of the healthiest insights into ministry in the contemporary church is that all ministers stand together with those they serve in the context of the body of the church. The priest is no longer the exalted figure removed from the rest of humankind, but rather a member of God's people—called indeed by Christ to a special role—but in need of support and encouragement and enlightenment from those he serves. The effective priest needs to be in touch.

I believe the same thing is true of the minister of music. If you are offering your talents to the church at the behest of the church and in the name of the church, you need to love the church as Christ loves the church, you need to be interested in the church, you need to be in touch with the church, especially with that portion of it that you are serving. This is just another way of formulating the Lord's basic command that we love our neighbor. We love our neighbor, among other ways, by listening to our neighbor, by being concerned with our neighbor's needs.

Doing what we are paid for is not enough in the horizontal dimension any more than it is in the vertical dimension. As ministers of the church we are called to be socially, spiritually, and ecclesially involved with our people. We don't just have a function. We have a ministry, and ministry implies concern for those we serve. It is as important for us to be aware of *whom* we are serving as it is to be aware of *what* we are there to do.

The first implication. We need to stay sensitive to the needs of our people. We need to listen to reaction, both good and bad. We will never know whether or not we are really helping people to pray unless we find ways to ask them. In the process we may find that there is a support for our ministry that we had not been aware of.

Second. Concern for the well-being of the people will probably demand openness on the part of pastoral musicians to different and changing musical tastes among the people. It's clear that Christmas midnight Mass and weekday liturgies and the occasional penance service require different musical aids to prayer. It is also clear that just as a people cannot be nourished by a steady diet of "Ave Verum" and "Panis Angelicus," so also they cannot be nourished by a steady diet of guitarists doing "Here We Are."

Liturgical presiders sometimes long for a change of pace, too. A couple of weeks ago at our national bishops' metteing, another bishop and I were talking about the limited range of music that we hear at confirmations. He said that by the end of the confirmation season he simply cannot "walk the barren desert," not even one more time. I should also tell you that sometimes I think that if I ever become pope I'm going to outlaw "Holy God, We Praise Thy Name." Maybe all this is merely a sign that there are occupational hazards to being bishop."

Third. As ministers of music you are not only charged with trying to respond to the different tastes people have and to the different needs they perceive. You are also charged with leading the people in their musical development. Our people deserve the good old stuff, but they also deserve the good new stuff, even if it's only new to *them*. The minister of music is not just a leader of prayer, but also a parish educator.

Fourth. A pastoral musician sometimes reaches a point when the people have received all that they can from his or her ministry, when there has been a settling down into routine (or into armed truce), when nothing more is happening or can happen. This occurs in priestly ministry, too, and pastors sometimes know that it's time to move on, both for the sake of their own development and for the sake of the people. Sometimes we owe the people a change of ministry. This isn't necessarily a sign of failure. It could be a sign of fulfillment.

We are now nearing the end of the "Sonata for Three Hands." I have tried to share with you some reflections about the meaning of ministry and about its vertical and horizontal dimensions. It is obvious to me that the three lines of the sonata are inseparable. We cannot separate prayer from concern for our neighbor, or ministry from prayer, or our responsibility to our neighbor from our ministerial responsibility to the church. It's all one. Each hand is playing all the time. It's not always clear which is playing the melody, but we need all three if our ministerial sonata is going to come out right.

I suspect that someone is by now accusing me of using a faulty metaphor. How can we speak of ministry as a sonata for three hands when we only have two, and when those hands are both busy most of the time? The answer is easy. Every real ministry demands both hands of the minister, but every ministry also includes the hand of God. I know mine does. And I'm sure yours does too. An awareness of the hand of the Lord needs to be part of the mind-set of every minister.

Finally, I want to offer a word of thanks . . . thanks for your concern for your ministry in the congregations you serve. Thanks for the music you—and the Lord—offer to his church.

SIX

THE IMPORTANCE OF PRAYER
FOR THE MUSICIAN

I would like to address you very simply, as a man, as your brother, as a believer in Jesus Christ, as a liturgist and musician, obviously, and as a pastor. I have no advice to give you. The liturgy is too intimately tied to culture, to language—especially song—and to the religious feelings of various human communities for a foreigner to be able to pass any judgment on the way they celebrate. But I do feel I can pass along to you some of my personal convictions.

I have worked for over forty years now to help my believing brothers and sisters pray in the liturgy. I have witnessed three very different periods.

Before the council we were searching enthusiastically, in the light of tradition, to rediscover the meaning of liturgy, and we were really struggling so that the faithful could participate. And then, a miracle happened: the Second Vatican Council. I had been convinced, during the first stage, that one day we would pray in our own mother tongue, but I thought that my grand nieces and nephews would see it.

The second stage was that of the reform. We worked according to the council's principles; we were reaping with joy that which we had sown; and the work spread to the entire church.

But a third period came, with its store of surprises. In practicing the new reformed rites, new needs seemed to appear, and these did not always correspond to what we had forseen. And to understand them, I had to unlearn everything I thought I knew.

And now I'm looking out for what tomorrow's liturgy might be like. I know that the most important still remains to be done; how each community may celebrate in truth the Risen Lord. To accomplish this, good, staunch principles and liturgical books cannot suffice. One must live, create, adjust with a deep sense of God and a great love for humanity. I suggest that we reflect on three aspects of our task as pastoral musicians. The first is to serve humanity for the service of God; the second, to serve the rites for the service of humanity; and third, to serve the music toward a new creation. These are not simple propositions. Each one of them carries antimonies and contrary forces. For life is a constant search for an equilibrium along all the forces that are pushing us forward.

Serve Others

First, we have to serve humanity for the service of God. I do not celebrate liturgy to make music that pleases *me*. I must search unceasingly for music that will help my fellow believers, gathered here together, to pray better. I must keep each and every one in mind, the young as well as the elderly; the cultivated as well as the more simple folk; those who are waiting to be helped by lots of joyous and expressive songs; but also those who will pray more profoundly, with less exuberant songs, and lots of silence.

I may not impose my tastes on anyone, but I must find for myself some taste in all I set about to do, in order to do it well. It is not easy to know what is good for a congregation. I have learned to be wary of individuals who react immediately to the first performance of a new song—"It's fantastic!" or, "It's horrible!" First of all, for one person who does react, what do the other ninety-nine think—those who never say anything? And then, if I question them to find out, what is said generally does not correspond well to what is experienced. The test of time is necessary to know whether a song is good for the prayer of a community. The opinions of experts are not enough. It's good music or it's bad music. Listen to them; but the sense of the Christian people, guided by the Holy Spirit, is *essential* to what is good according to the *sensus communis ecclesiae*.

It is still more difficult to know if a repertoire or a certain way of singing in the liturgy is good—that is, if it really and truly corresponds to the spirit of the Gospel that we are proclaiming. What does this Gospel say? "Blessed are the poor"; "Blessed are those who cry"; "Blessed are those who are persecuted for justice." Is it possible to announce the justice of the Kingdom with exclusively intimate, pietistic texts, and with sentimental melodies? Are we really poor at heart, capable of hearing the Gospel, if we copy the kitsch of the mass media, and the false luxury of a consumer society? In celebrating ourselves, are we truly celebrating the God of Jesus Christ, dead and risen? Shall we have the courage to tear ourselves away for all that must perish and thrust ourselves into the world that is coming?

It is not my task to flatter the congregation, but to help it die and rise again in Jesus Christ. It will be like the little scroll that John had to eat, according to the Apocalypse—sweet as honey in his mouth, but how bitter to the stomach! Beauty, like truth, seduces and terrifies all at once. I serve humanity, of course, but in order that they may celebrate the God of Jesus Christ and no other god, and that they may find their way to the Kingdom.

Serve the Rites

Second, we have to serve the rites in order to serve humanity. You will recall the old theological saying, *sacramenta propter homines*. Literally, it means "the sacraments are for people." But I would translate: "If there are rites and liturgy at all, it is because people need them." They are not for God—he does not need our rites. The rites give glory to God only in the measure that humanity is sanctified. There is a phrase, the phrase that Jesus quoted most often in the Gospels: "It is love that I want, not your sacrifices." Jesus was scathing in his condemnation of ritualism, whether the Sabbath, or the temple (it was precisely because of his attitude about the temple that Jesus was condemned to death). But the Holy Spirit is given to humanity only through signs and symbols. The rite is not an action by which we have a grasp on God, but that place where we welcome the gift of his grace, through the beautiful and wonderful things of this world. "No one, unless he be born again of water and of the Spirit . . ."; "Take and eat of this bread. You will be my Body."

There is a liturgy in the church, then, with rites that are not ritualism, but effective signs of life in the Holy Spirit, and of worship in spirit and truth, which is nothing other than offering one's life out of love. There are no other standards for our music.

Three reflections come to mind. First, you must take the symbolic rites seriously. You must enter into the liturgy with your whole being, your whole voice, your whole body, all of your feelings, your whole heart, your whole spirit. When one is animating the liturgy, when one is singing, or presiding, it is difficult to concentrate totally on what one is doing. St. Augustine himself admitted that he sometimes felt torn between the seduction of overly beautiful melodies and prayer. Personally, this is not my greatest difficulty; I was aware of this when I was in the seminary. When I entered the Society of Jesus, I made a single very great sacrifice that cost me plenty: it was that of never again making music. Then music was given back to me in the Society, and God freed me from this inner conflict between music and prayer. But I especially had to learn not to be preoccupied, when celebrating, with musical technique, the order of the rites, or the few words I would have to improvise. The organist playing a Bach prelude has to forget technique. It's impossible to pray if I'm thinking of something else. There's only one solution: to be confident in the rites, in the gesture, in the act.

If, when I arrive to celebrate the Mass, I am very tired by my work and all the phone calls and I am distracted, then, as I enter, I put my trust in my feet and in my hands. And what was in conflict is welded back together. For if I sing, I become praise; if I recite a psalm, I become the psalm; if I raise my hands, I become dance. And if I eat, I become the Body of Christ. But for this, the solution is never to escape myself with my mind; it is to do very well with my body. The dancer defies gravity by experiencing it in his limbs; the liturgy is done with the hands, the feet, the ears, the eyes, and the mouth. The Holy Spirit cannot act anywhere else.

The second reflection that comes to mind is simplicity. Simplicity alone allows the Holy Spirit to act in the liturgy. Complication, effort, challenge—these things can destroy the spirit of celebration. When St. Augustine spoke of the Christian liturgy, he said that the pagans had very complicated rites, which they didn't understand, and which they performed mechanically. We Christians, however, had very few rites, and they were very simple and within the grasp of each one of us. Blessed were those times of St. Augustine, because in the meantime our liturgy has become very complicated, overcrowded—too many words, too many songs, too many botched gestures, too many devalued symbols.

Do less to do better. After all, we can't do everything. When you go to a good restaurant, are you obliged to eat every dish on the menu? I am pleased that our Holy Mother the Church has restored to us a very rich liturgy; but we must know how to use it. I don't want to get indigestion at any restaurant! The problem is not one of reforming the liturgy all over again, but how to use well what is available to us now, without necessarily being obliged to consume the entire menu.

Third reflection: it is impossible to know what is good or bad without having tasted it. The principles are useful, but in the life of the Spirit, they are not sufficient. Only experimentation, and our discernment from experience, can guide us. And at this period of the liturgical reform, experiment is irreplacable. Liturgists don't know in advance what is good. Believing communities must discover it for themselves. This is how liturgy has grown in the church.

But what then of liturgical law, obedience, and His Excellency the Bishop? I am a Jesuit, and I made vows of obedience. But the worst of all obedience is that which is perfectly content to execute. I must do my best to do what must be done. Three things are necessary. First, we have to know well what the church really wants us to do. For that, we have to study and reflect; it's one of the things that's most lacking at present. Second, we must be confident in the essential symbols—sharing bread, singing, bowing, and so forth. Third, we must experiment with various ways of doing things to see which ones are fruitful.

We must not turn the liturgy upside down. Rather, against a very stable background, we must make small variations to see if it's good. Risks are involved, but who can live without risks? We can always learn from our mistakes. Are we afraid? Of whom? Not of God! The only thing we should fear is that we might prefer law over charity.

Serve Music

To conclude, how can we serve music toward the new creation? Am I really at the service of music? I am in the service of God and my brother and sister believers, not music. Music, like all the rites, is for humanity. However, reality is not so simple.

I like very much to work with my hands—carpentry work, for example. One of the most important tasks is making the tool. You must adjust the tool, take it in hand, get accustomed to using it so that the work might be useful and beautiful.

So it is in the liturgy. We must prepare with love and care the symbolic tools, which are the words, things, sounds. I know the risks of involving myself with music. Father Jungmann has spoken of it as the "terrible centrifugal force of music in the history of the liturgy." I know of its ravages in history. I still see some of them today: the concert Mass, the jam-session Mass, the "happening" Mass. I notice cantors and organists who like to show off, and congregations that can never have their fill of the folk song idiom. It makes me dream of a musical fast, so that we may pray.

But the solution does not lie in suppressing the music; I absolutely need it. Even during long hours of silent prayer, when I pray with the Jesus Prayer—that marvelous tool of prayer, "Jesus, Son of David, have mercy on me, a sinner"—I have a little inner melody that helps me extend the words.

I would wish that in the liturgy there might not always be the maximum of decibels, the greatest possible number of voices, the richest possible harmonies; but that in contrast to these moments filled with music—because meaning always comes out of contrast—there would be an absolutely naked melody, without harmony or accompaniment. Then I can adore.

That I might have a psalm with very few notes, and a song in a subdued voice. For the Spirit awaits my emptiness in order to fill it. The veritable artist is one who can make emptiness. The musician doesn't use all the sounds of nature; rather, the musician chooses, and between the notes there is emptiness. The painter reveals that which the eye has not yet seen. The poet speaks words that have never been uttered, but the poet uses very few words, and between the words the poet leaves emptiness. The musician must make heard that which has never been heard. When I say this, I don't mean that we must write music that no one has ever written, but that it must be done in such a way that it appears to be born *now* of the Spirit.

So may the liturgy of today make room for true artists, not only babblers who are forever in need of explaining things, not only for endless projection of slides, not only for guitar strummers and amplifiers, but especially for those who, with fewer words, allow us to hear the eternal Word in the silence, who let us contemplate in the icon the glory of the Invisible, who make audible the harmony of the new heavens, and the new Earth, this wonderful miracle of love that is unison between God and humanity. May our music reveal to humanity this wisdom of the mystery of God, of which St. Paul spoke to the Corinthians: "We proclaim that which the ear has not heard: all that God has prepared for those who love him."

Charles Conley

SEVEN

DESCRIBING THE PASTORAL MUSICIAN'S ROLE

Most people probably have no idea what is meant by "pastoral musician." The phrase is rather new, and many are still saying "church musician" or "liturgical musician"; yet there is wisdom in using the term "pastoral." The word itself refers to an area of study within the field of theology. In its origins, during the eighteenth century, pastoral theology was concerned with aiding clergy in their day-to-day work as pastors—offering them helpful guidance in matters of preaching, liturgizing, counseling, and administration. Recently, however, the area of pastoral theology has expanded and developed so much that its concerns are concerns for the entire church, not just its ordained ministers.

The question faced by today's pastoral theologian is: "What should the church's course of action be at this time?" Vatican II was concerned with the same question. Being a truly pastoral council, Vatican II was concerned with the question of how we as Christians could best be church and live out the church's mission in our contemporary world.

Pastoral theology addresses issues on the basis of two sources of investigation: the church's past experience and its present situation. If, for example the question is one of parish size, pastoral theology first examines how Christians have grouped themselves in times past. What has brought them together? When did the parish structure emerge? Under what historical conditions did this structuring come about?

Next, pastoral theology studies Christians' present-day experience, with questions such as: "Is the present parish structure keeping alive all aspects of Christian life that brought believers together throughout the church's history? Does the parish structure need to be refined, or is there a need for altogether new models?

This investigation leads to a dialogue which, combined with reflection and interaction, allows the pastoral theologian to determine how the church should act and proceed in its mission here and now. And it is precisely this process of dialogue, reflection, and interaction that is necessary for the work of the musician who wishes to be called "pastoral."

There are three dimensions of the pastoral musician that must be held in constant dialogue with one another: the pastoral musician as a member of the Christian community; the pastoral musician as a student of the liturgy; and the pastoral musician as a professional musician. The dialogue is ongoing both among ourselves in the field of pastoral music and within each of us as we minister.

MEMBER OF THE CHRISTIAN COMMUNITY

Though many begin with the professional aspect of the pastoral musician's role, the pastoral musician should be considered first as a person of faith, a Christian—an active member of a faith community. The pastoral musician is, first of all, a person who has been converted to the life of our brother Jesus, and who is trying to live the pattern of his death and resurrection, not alone, but together with other Christians. Christianity began and will culminate with the experience of the risen Jesus. We, as members of the Christian community at work in the world today, are not cut off from our ancestry, or from the initial experience of the chosen witnesses. Christ is forever present with his people. His presence has continued to unfold for each generation, and is present for us as well. To be effective pastoral musicians, aware of what our ministry really means, we must be thoroughly convinced of Christ's presence. Furthermore, we must be convinced of the primary place of this presence: that the risen Christ is fundamentally present in the Christian community gathered for prayer.

Article 7 of the Constitution on the Sacred Liturgy states: "Christ is always present in his Church, especially in her liturgical celebrations . . . He is present when the Church prays and sings." Before we even hear him speak to us in the word proclaimed, before we take and bless, break and share the bread, the Lord "is present when the Church prays and sings." The other ways in which the Lord is present—in the word proclaimed, in the food shared—"are for the sake of his presence in his people" (Nicholas Lash, *His Presence in the World*, p. 142).

Why is it so crucial that we as pastoral musicians be convinced of the presence of Christ *in us*? Because, as pastoral musicians, we minister to this presence of Christ in the gathered community. In choosing the people's song, in leading and arranging their musical prayer, we are giving shape to the way this presence of Christ is realized by the community. The presiding minister is responsible for making the community aware of themselves as the people of God, the place of Christ's presence. Musicians are responsible for doing the same through musical prayer. It is the touchstone of our ministry.

Remember the words of Pius X: "The faithful gather to gain the true Christian spirit from its first and indispensable source: the active participation in the sacred mysteries and the public and solemn prayer of the Church" (*Motu proprio*, no. 6). The "true Christian spirit" is the spirit of Christ; and the key to becoming aware of this presence of Christ is participation.

In 1965 Robert Lechner wrote in *Worship* (vol. 39, p. 261):

> It is not chance that the overall, the all embracing word that we use to speak of the act that is proper to the assembly is not love, not knowing, not sensing, but *participation*. An assembly only exists when a group within the Church is actually sharing. And the goal of this participation is the realization of a *presence*. We might say that the grace proper to the assembly is the heightened presence of Christ in the midst of God's people. And the more deep the presence of Christ, the more the assembly is the place where salvation is going on and glory is given to the Father.

Since by now we have been working at it for some time, we know what enters into obtaining effective participation in musical liturgy: trained musicians, choral groups and cantors, music that is worthy of participation, sensible pedagogy, good musical instruments. All these are necessary and vital to achieving participation. If all this musicianship and pedagogy is to bear fruit, however, there needs to be the desire for *community*.

The entire musical team—clergy, religious educators, musicians, parish council—shares the task of introducing parishioners to want to become a *community* of believers, involved in one another's lives and in the mission of the church. The pastoral musician cannot hope for participation in musical prayer if the whole leadership of the parish is not concerned with raising the communal consciousness of the believers. All who lead must want to form the parish into a community concerned about one another's faith-life; into a people who want to take part in Christ's work of salvation.

—The reason why I as a worshiper should join in singing the entrance song has to do with my ability to recognize the Lord present in my brothers and sisters.

—The reason I want to acclaim the Lamb of God as the bread is broken, and sing with my brother and sister believers as the eucharist is shared, has everything to do with breaking open my life day to day in deeds of loving service for others, seeking to build one communion of love.

—The reason I want to express the Christian faith with hearty and vigorous hymns, sung loudly with a whole congregation, has much to do with taking an interest in adult religious education, with teaching my children truly Christian values, or perhaps with getting involved in the formation of the adult catechumens.

Pastoral musicians cannot go it alone. Our work is part of the entire pastoral effort to build vital parish communities. Each one involved in parish ministry must understand church as the communion of God's people shared faith and prayer, shared fellowship and responsibility, shared mission.

The first priority in the process of dialogue for pastoral musicians is that they be members of the community, and know from first-hand experience—their own lives and relationships with fellow believers—the daily struggles, failures, successes, joys and sufferings of Christians. Just as the priest must be immersed in the life of the community and be a member of that community if he is to lead their prayer and interpret Scripture for them, so too the pastoral musician must be in touch with the community's life if the musician is to be a leader of prayer and know what music and text will help this people realize that they are Christ's presence in the world.

LITURGICAL UNDERSTANDING

The second dimension of the pastoral musician is liturgical understanding. It is becoming increasingly clear that pastoral musicians should know more about the liturgy and how Christians have prayed communally over the years. If our present practice is to be honestly Christian and in continuity with the whole tradition of the worshiping church, we need to understand this tradition. Without a knowledge of liturgical principles and history, how can we make the right choices in liturgical planning and know the difference between merely tinkering and actually helping to lead the people's prayer appropriately? It is not the prayer of a liturgy committee, but the prayer of the Christian community that concerns us.

In the 1950s it was enough for the church musician to know the *Ordo*: what piece of music is sung at each point in the liturgy; in the 1960s it was enough to find simple vernacular settings of the Ordinary and Proper, plus a few hymns; in the 1970s a thorough knowledge of the principles of Music in Catholic Worship sufficed, and efforts to incorporate them are a continuing project. Today the pastoral musician must become a student of liturgy— really come to learn everything possible about the roots of our worship, its development, and even our mistaken practices in the past, so that we do not return to them again.

The pastoral musician does not have to be a liturgist, but rather a student of the liturgy. Part of our professional competence as pastoral musicians necessitates an ongoing study of the liturgy. It should become more common for church musicians to take paid summer sabbaticals in order to study core courses in liturgy. It may well be that the pastoral musician of the future will be the one person in the parish who is most knowledgeable in the area of liturgy; in some places this is already the case.

MUSICIANSHIP

In 1967 Sr. Theophane Hytrek wrote: "Until the hierarchy and clergy recognize that the position of a music director is a highly specialized area requiring special competencies and training, music in our churches will remain in a sad state of affairs" ("Facing Reality," in *Crisis in Church Music*, The Liturgical Conference, p. 99).

As church, we have begun to break out of the mentality that a self-trained piano player or a guitarist who can strum three chords in two keys can really do the job of a church musician. The use of non-trained non-musicans supports the notion that music is peripheral to the liturgy; that all we need is some kind of music in the background to fill in the empty spaces or cover over the moments of procession during the liturgy. As Robert Batastini once said, "Basically, where the musician is incompetent, the congregation is simply not singing" (*Pastoral Music* 3:4, p. 42).

A parish needs a professional who knows what good music is, and how to make music that is good; a person who can discern from the wealth of available music the compositions that have substance, and the ones that are superficial. A parish needs a musician who can not only play Bach with articulation in even time, but also dynamically lead a congregation in its song.

To be a professional musician, hours of self-discipline and hard work are necessary. We are continually growing in our art and musical proficiency. The church must protect our creative and musical abilities, and allow us the space and time we need to keep our musicianship alive and well.

The question of whether the church will seriously pursue musical quality in its worship life is largely one of salary. Fewer people are seeking church music as a profession because the salaries are so low. Unless the administrators of our parishes fully address the problem of equitable salary for church musicians, we will drive musical professionalism out of the church, rather than welcoming and encouraging musical artists, the very people our worship life so desperately needs.

The article "Civil Rights for Church Musicians (*The American Organist*, May 1980) by Maureen Morgan of the American Guild of Organists goes one step beyond the question of fair wages. She addresses the issue of job benefits for church musicians, benefits normally taken for granted by most other jobholders: Social Security, medical coverage, pensions, and unemployment compensation. Clergymen have all these benefits. Church musicians, also servants of the Lord and of his church, have a right to share the same benefits as the ordained.

As professional musicians, we must always strive for musical excellence yet be keenly aware that professionalism and artistic technique are not for self-aggrandizement but for the people's prayer. This means that because we are members of the community, there are times when we have to let our professional musicianship be tempered by the needs of the community.

Accordingly, it is extremely important that as pastoral musicians we possess simple skills of communication with people, be they clergy, liturgical committees, or the parishioners themselves. A little human psychology can go a long way. For example, the *way* we tell a bride and a bride's mother that the march from *Lohengrim* and the popular song "Evergreen" will not assist the prayer of the marriage liturgy, is extremely important. Saying "No! You can't do that!" will naturally arouse anxiety, whereas taking the time to gently suggest, explain, and persuade, will make all the difference in the world.

In a past issue of *Pastoral Music* (1:4, p. 20) Aidan Kavanagh complained that liturgists and musicians have gone their separate ways:

> Not only has each of us suffered because of this . . . the communities of faith we each would serve have been stunningly pauperized by our respective monologues with ourselves . . . Neither of our respective gifts by themselves will make them a people vibrant in the faith that may be the world's salvation.

There are three instances in which our liturgical sensibility and knowledge can especially affect how we expend our efforts musically: the responsorial psalm, the eucharistic prayer, and the *fractio* or the breaking of the bread. In the General Instruction on the Liturgy of the Hours we read:

> The psalms are not readings; nor are they prayers composed after the fashion of a collect . . . in view of their literary character, they are rightly called in the Hebrew language *tehillim*, that is, "canti-

cles of praise"; and in the Greek language *psalmoi*, that is, "songs to be sung to the sound of the psaltery." Truly there is a certain musical character inherent in all the psalms which determines the proper manner of their delivery. (no. 103).

Liturgically, the responsorial psalm demands to be sung. The dynamic proper to the liturgy of the word is the proclamation of God's word to his people, evoking their heartfelt response. To have a lector merely recite the psalm after having already spoken the reading disrupts the experience of proclamation and response, and suffocates the listeners with all too many words. If a cantor, however, comes before the assembly and leads them in sung response, the liturgy of the word comes alive because, as the Instruction continues: ". . . though [the psalm] most certainly represents a text to the mind of the faithful, it is designed more to move the hearts of those singing and listening, and indeed of those accompanying it 'on the psaltery and harp'."

The second area requiring greater musical attention is the eucharistic prayer. If we truly believe that this prayer is at the heart of our eucharist, simply inserting sung acclamations here and there will not do. Composers are challenged to work together to produce musical settings of the eucharistic prayers; through-composed settings that will allow the prayer to be experienced as one liturgical unity, one unified prayer—from the introductory dialogue to the doxology-amen.

But eucharistic prayers will not be sung if we do not have priests who can sing them. The real challenge, in all seriousness, is to train our clergy to sing. Years ago every newly ordained priest was prepared to sing a Latin preface at his First Mass. If your clergy cannot sing, offer to work with them. Of course, our clergy will have to meet us at least halfway on this difficult task.

The breaking of the bread is the third area of consideration. The ancient pattern of the eucharistic ritual, following the Lord's own action, is fourfold: take the bread, bless it, break it, and share it. The third act—the significant symbolic action of breaking the bread—is still quite often lost from the view and participation of the people. This is due in great part to the fact that we still use hosts, even though the General Instruction of the Roman Missal states: "The nature of the sign demands that the material for eucharistic celebration appear as actual food" (no. 283). This problem should be the concern of the church as a whole if the human experience of a meal is to be realized within the eucharist, and if the action of the *fractio* is to be a significant moment.

Integral to the liturgical act of the bread-breaking is the people's participation by *watching* while the bread is being broken. As musicians, we can encourage the congregation to observe the action and not have their eyes on a printed page during this moment by using the liturgical-musical form of the litany, which invites the congregation's response with ease and simplicity. The people's experience of the breaking of the bread can be enhanced by a musical setting of the Lamb of God.

The many years and countless hours we have spent training to be musicians have finally made artists of us. The liturgy desperately needs the gift not only of our musical creativity, but of the larger artistic sensitivity and insight that we can bring to liturgical planning; a kind of intuition about designing a liturgy that is truly an action of beauty. Music in Catholic Worship states:

> To celebrate the liturgy means to do the action or perform the sign in such a way that the full meaning and impact shine forth in clear and compelling fashion. Since these signs are vehicles of communication and instruments of faith, they must be simple and comprehensible. Since they are directed to fellow human beings, they must be humanly attractive. They must be meaningful and appealing to the body of worshippers or they will fail to stir up faith and men [and women] will fail to worship the Father. (no. 7).

So often our liturgies are not humanly attractive experiences because they lack artistic unity. Instead of being felt as one dramatic action of love and praise, having continuity and a flow and a rhythm of their own, our rituals at times seem to be a compilation of disjointed parts, a patchwork quilt rather than an integrated fabric.

Liturgical planning needs the insights of an artist who can receive from the liturgy committee what they have planned, ponder it awhile, and then balance the moments of word, song and silence, gestures, action, and mood into a unified whole.

The composer must take a similar approach before completing a work of art. The composition is evaluated from the standpoint of how each musical element affects the other: melody line, key placement, rhythm, chord progression, dynamics of interpretation. But then the piece must also be considered as a whole, from beginning to end. Is there a unity within the composition that holds it together, a continuity of style and form? Is there a sense of completeness and resolution, a feeling of satisfaction from this musical experience?

The evaluative process has to be part of liturgy planning, and it must take place before the liturgy is set in motion. If we as musicians, as artists in residence, know thoroughly the innate rhythm of the liturgy itself—the peak moments the highs and lows of the liturgical action—we can bring our artistic sensitivity to bear on ritual planning and achieve worship that is an artistic expression of the community's faith. Our worship will be a thing of beauty not for its own sake, but for the sake of becoming aware of Christ's splendid and holy presence dwelling in us.

As pastoral musicians we have a particular role in the process of transforming men and women into other Christs. Ildefonse Herwegen, O.S.B., the great abbot of Maria Laach, in an address entitled "The Art-Principle of the Liturgy," stated a challenge to artists in 1912 that still holds today:

> The liturgy is . . . the life-breath of the church, the very spirit and life of Christ who is the prototype of the entire cosmos of creation. Hence it must somehow reflect the splendor of the eternal Word, it must contain the element of beauty . . . The purpose of the Christian religion is . . . to form mankind . . . in the likeness of Christ . . . to sanctify, to spiritualize, to deify mankind, to bring us as transfigured Christians to the transfigured Christ. This is accomplished . . . through the liturgy. The purpose of the liturgy is the transfiguration of human souls. It is this transcendent purpose that has brought out the inherent beauty of the liturgy and made it a consummate work of art.

Marie Therese Kalb

EIGHT

DIRECTIVES TO A PASTORAL MUSICIAN

To determine the principles for uncovering that correct piece of music, we must know our purpose, our goal as church musicians. What is our particular function and role as the faith community gathers on Sunday morning? What is our reason for being there—as pastoral musicians? Our goal as pastoral musicians is to use our gifts to empower for worship—to enable, to cause worship to happen, to help create an encounter between God and his people—in ourselves first and foremost and then in others— in the celebrant and the congregation.

The American bishops have said that "music is a bridge to a faith—as well as an expression of it." The music of the entrance hymn, for example, accompanies the priest and ministers as they come into the building for worship. It is easy to enter a building; to walk with our minds and hearts into the spirit of liturgical celebration is more difficult. Our goal as pastoral musicians is to help people do just that.

We are still very near the beginning of a new and creative phase in the realm of church music. Sometimes we may be tempted to excuse ourselves by talking about the present "crisis" in church music. We may try to cover up our own impotence by complaining about a general loss of quality in church music. We may claim that we cannot create or perform the kind of music that seems to be required because of our loyalty to our musical profession. What principles can guide us in finding the correct piece of music? In accord with Music in Catholic Worship, the discussion is divided into three parts: pastoral principles, liturgical principles, and musical principles.

PASTORAL PRINCIPLES

What are some of the pastoral principles that will help us in our task? The first is very simple: *unite and inspire*. An effective piece of music has the power to unite the worshiping community. People remain separate unless the group expresses its unity in a common action that signifies its reason for assembling, for coming together. Perhaps the most significant of all the actions a congregation performs is singing. Individuals who were previously a crowd can become a faith community through song. Another way in which music has pastoral significance is that it has the power to inspire. Music also has the power to create celebration, to add solemnity and dignity to simply human actions. It is hard to imagine a celebration of any kind that does not have music as an integral part. The first principle asks, can this music unite? Can it inspire with beauty? Can it add solemnity? Can it create something?

The second principle is to *consider the congregation*. The "best" piece of music is rarely the one that is "best" in itself—or the "best" in a particular book. Rather, it is the one that is best for the particular group celebrating in a particular place, on a particular occasion. The Constitution on the Sacred Liturgy made a decisive step in the history of active participation of the people when it stated, "By way of promoting active participation, the people should be encouraged to take part by means of acclamations, responses, psalmody, antiphons, and songs" (no. 30). The 1967 Instruction on Sacred Music applies this directive. It states: "In selecting the kind of sacred music to be used, whether it be for the choir or for the people, the ability of those who are to sing the music must be taken into account" (no. 9). In addition, the church, for the first time in history, in 1973, issued a special document to tell us that children's Masses should be different from Masses in which the majority in the congregation are adults.

Previously the rubrics had never really considered the worshiping community. The church's directives were more concerned with whether the singing conformed to the letter of the law, not the spirit of the people. Christians throughout the world—regardless of culture, background, or desire—were to sing the same Gregorian melodies. Most of us can readily recall the triple alleluia from the Paschal Vigil. The Christians of India would much prefer to use the five notes of their pentatonic system, which is more beautiful and meaningful to their ears. From the societies of Africa there is a plea for more rhythm. They want to sing to the resurrected Christ, but not with an alleluia that to them resembles a funeral march. Even in America, in the culture of the 1940s, we couldn't manage to sing this alleluia together. Instead of expressing the union of hearts and the glorious triumph of the Lord, our voices slid over the notes as they would over ice. Yet, the rubrics said to *all* of us—Indians, Africans, Americans—that our cultures made no difference. Sing as written. This is the glorious heritage of our faith. Now the church's official documents are saying to consider the congregation. Choose the alleluia that will best help to unite this particular group in a full-throated joyous acclamation of Christ.

The third pastoral principle is to choose and serve the text. The text must express Christian truths. Down through the ages and even today people have learned much of their theology—their faith—through hymnody. Popular hymns have played a great part in the religious reforms of Luther, Calvin, Wesley, and in the Catholic Counter-Reformation. As we select our music, we must ask what it is saying. If it is other than liturgical text, is it communicating God's word—the truths of our faith?

Also, music must serve the text. This principle goes back to Pius X, who stated in his *Motu proprio* of 1903 that the "chief duty [of music] is to clothe the liturgical text . . . with suitable melody, its object is to make that text more efficacious" (Instruction on Sacred Music, no. 1). The principle that music is the text's servant, its backdrop, is reiterated in all of the recent directives on sacred music.

Liturgical language does not present the mystery in the same way as descriptive language does. It endows the mystery with its own special operativity—and somehow the faith community is caught up, reliving the mystery about which it sings or speaks. Faith takes up this language and gives it its own efficacy. Language is to faith a kind of structuring field that allows faith to express itself. Liturgical language is the location of Christ's presence for us in the present day of celebration.

Music is the servant of the word. Does the text communicate to this particular congregation, with their unique culture, social status, ages, and background? Will it communicate the appropriate message, convey the proper attitude, engender the spirit of this particular celebration?

The final pastoral principle is to *nourish with repetition and variety*. We have all experienced the devastating effect that monotonous repetition can have on the life of faith. Can you imagine what would happen to your relationship with your best friend if suddenly you started repeating the same formulas several times a day for twenty to thirty minutes each time—for a period of two to three years? Of course, there has to be a certain amount of repetition to *enable* the congregation to participate. Long-range planning can help ensure that good hymns get repeated but also that there is room for newness, creativity, freshness. The music we sing must somehow capture our attention, somehow express the sentiments in our hearts and address the situations of our world as it exists today. Our faith will be nourished with sufficient repetition to ensure participation and sufficient variety to lend inspiration.

LITURGICAL PRINCIPLES

What are the liturgical principles for uncovering the correct piece of music? If you were to consider just one aspect of selecting a particular piece of music, obey the ministerial function. Like the service performed by the good servant, each part of the liturgical celebration—each piece of music— must fulfill the role assigned to it by the liturgy itself. This "golden rule" as stated in the 1967 Instruction on Sacred Music reads: "The proper arrangement of a liturgical celebration . . . demands that the meaning and proper nature of each part and of each chant be carefully observed" (no. 6).

The principle is one of making it more true—liturgically—by *having or not having a particular piece of music*. In the past ten years, liturgists and musicians have been teaching the liturgical function of music in such a way that people today are beginning to long for an Introit that is really an entrance song—or for a Kyrie that is really a litany of supplication; a Holy, Holy that really expresses the acclamation of people in festive celebration. An immense thirst has arisen in the church for liturgical authenticity.

An important element of this ministerial function is the very structure or form that a musical composition takes. The structures vary and are influenced by the type of liturgical action as well as by the meaning of the text. Each part has its own particular appearance, its own lyric movement, its own liturgical personality. Experts among pastoral musicians establish the following categories: acclamations and dialogues; responsorial psalms; the Lord Have Mercy and Lamb of God litanies; the processionals—entrance, gospel, preparation of the gifts, communion; hymns of glory—the sequence, thanksgiving hymn, closing hymn; the profession of faith; and the readings. For example, the Holy, Holy is an acclamation; it must therefore be "acclaimed." The Sanctus of the Gregorian Mass VIII (*De Angelis*), is beautiful, but lengthy in style. This Sanctus was most fitting for the liturgy before Vatican II when the priest continued the eucharistic prayer in a low voice; but now a short more acclamatory Holy, Holy should be chosen.

In the past, it was not uncommon to find composers using the same melody for the Kyrie and the Ite Missa Est. Should we really dismiss the faith community in the same musical style and with the same melody/harmony as that used to implore God's mercy? The ministerial functions of these two parts are obviously different. If a certain melody, rhythm, or harmony is unique in its beauty, should it not be reserved for one special function only? The ministerial function is the fundamental criterion from which have arisen the best of current liturgical reforms. It is the starting point from which we will be able to grow in intelligent understanding of the liturgy and its potential.

A second liturgical principle is to *observe varied roles*. We musicians were often limited in the past to a schola or a choir. Today, a great variety of vistas are open to us—look at the musical dimensions of the worshiping assembly. If ninety percent of our investment of time and energy is in people, we have a resource that keeps growing.

First of all, there is the *priest-celebrant,* who, depending on his musical giftedness, has definite parts he can sing.

The *cantor's* ministerial role is all too little developed as of yet by the average parish. This person can have a tremendous impact in empowering for worship. The responsorial psalm, for example, is an integral part of the liturgy of the word. Clearly, we need to develop an appreciation for the richness of the psalms—that the proclamation of our faith is not a task or a burdensome string of words to be rattled off after the first reading. Through the response, the community's faith life is inspired. It is the expression of praise and thanks for the *mirabilia Dei*—the marvels of God as recalled in his word. The form of the responsorial psalm should be exactly the same as that of the literary form of the psalm it represents. Some psalms are supplications; others are hymns; still others are lamentations or joyful acclamations. Particular psalms are chosen because of specific reference to them in the reading that precedes or follows them, or to illustrate what was proclaimed in the word even though there is no specific reference, or perhaps because of the particular liturgical season or cycle being celebrated. In any case, a good cantor can do much to make the responsorial psalm come alive, to be an integral and meaningful part of the word. A cantor can also greatly enrich a communion processional, or lead the plea for mercy or Lamb of God litanies.

Regarding the *congregation,* Lucien Deiss says: "As a general principle, never have others do what the congregation can do for itself."

Finally, there is the *choir.* The General Instruction indicates a dual function for the choir; to ensure the proper performance of the parts that belong to it; and to encourage the active participation of the faithful in singing. Needless to say, the choir should sing with such perfection that the people will yearn to tell them, "We want to sing like you—what you do is so beautiful that we are enchanted, inspired, empowered for worship by it." On the other hand, if the choir's singing of their choice of music is as dreary as a rainy day, its singing is not only invalid on the musical level, but it should be condemned liturgically as well, for the choir is not accomplishing its ministerial role.

Let there be different roles. We need each of them to provide for the lavishness of God's giftedness to his people, to provide a great variety of approaches to empowering all for worship.

A third liturgical principle, flowing directly from the second, is to *vary the format*. It is fitting that the format of the celebration and the degrees of participation in it should be varied as much as possible, according to the solemnity of the day and the nature of the congregation present. There is a recognizable difference between times when the faith community gathers to celebrate the great high feast of the Lord's resurrection, or the coming of the Spirit, and when it is a simple Sunday in Ordinary Time.

The final liturgical principle is to *continue to grow*. Vatican II stated that "composers and singers must be given genuine liturgical training." The 1967 Instruction develops this even more forcefully. "Besides musical formation, suitable liturgical and spiritual formation must also be given to the members of the choir, so that the proper performance of their liturgical role will not only enhance the beauty of the celebration and be an excellent example to the faithful, but will bring spiritual benefit to the choir members themselves" (no. 24). We have a long way to go in the area of spiritual and liturgical formation—to make the words of the Instruction come true—so that "proper performance of our liturgical role will bring spiritual benefit, will empower ourselves, and everyone else, for worship."

MUSICAL PRINCIPLES

In the area of musical principles, *watch* your priorities. Participation supersedes perfection. David Power says: "Desire for the ideal should not lead us to the suppression of the real." There is a real danger for us professionals. "Music is an art," we will say. "Our congregations are made up of musical barbarians." The aim of liturgy, however, is not to promote the musical education of the people in order to obtain a better musical rendition. The church is a mystery of salvation—not a conservatory of music.

The people's singing is always valuable if it expresses, according to the liturgical rules, the participation of the baptized in the worship of the Father. It is unthinkable to deny the people this right merely for esthetic reasons. Among the holy people there will always be voices that quaver and bellow; others that go flat. The most important and essential thing is the participation in the mystery being celebrated. Granted, participation will be enhanced if people can sing—and sing better. The goal toward which we want to move is not to promote the quality of the singing but to foster the people's participation—and this can be accomplished through improved singing. Liturgy needs art to express itself more fully.

The sound of the congregation singing has a special quality all its own. We cannot judge the people with the same criteria used for a choir. When the whole church is singing, no one is listening except God. When there is a union of all voices—good, bad, vibratos, and flats—something happens, a miracle that you can understand only if you have ever sung in such a group or had the honor of accompanying a faith community as its members proclaim their faith and joy.

The second musical principle is to *challenge realistically*. Musicians should never underestimate people's musical potential or their artistic sense. Our faith cannot be subjected to kindergarten-level repertoire. In order to foster singing among your people, begin with the simple and progress from there. The rungs of a ladder should not be so high that they cannot be reached, but only just low enough for everyone to begin to climb up to new possibilities.

The third musical principle is to *communicate in the present*. It is a challenging and exciting era for pastoral musicians. Part of our task is to adapt the church's liturgy to present-day people—to present-day demands. For the person who peers into the future, a look backward into the past can be filled with peace and understanding. Clearly, our style of celebrating the Mass has changed considerably within recent years, and our style of music is certainly not the same as it was in the sixteenth century—or in any other century.

In pondering this area, we inevitably run into the question of secular music versus sacred music. Archbishop Rembert Weakland holds that "if history teaches us anything about the conflict we constantly pose for ourselves between sacred and secular music, it is this: the most fruitful period was that in which such a distinction did not exist." Gerardus van der Leeuw prophetically said this years ago when he wrote:

> In the history of church music, new life always unfolds when a strong awareness of being called by God and being bound to him is combined with the determination to go out into the world and praise God. For then the folk song entered the church, then the world seemingly conquered the altar; in reality the altar conquered the world. Then songs resounded, those "new songs" which ascended to God's throne when he had given them to us in his grace.

Our music, if it is authentic, must communicate to the people here and now. Some hymn texts still being used are archaic. As a basic principle, when you try to uncover that right piece of music, ask yourself whether it can communicate, whether it can speak to the heart of modern-day women and men.

Our final guideline for pastoral musicians is to work as a team. Perhaps the best assurance that many (or all) of the preceding principles will be operative is for the pastoral musician to be part of the viable planning group. If your parish has a liturgy committee, be an important and integral part of it. If not, consider organizing such a group. Take the initiative and help your pastor to realize the importance of having such a number of people working together so that the liturgy will empower all for worship. Work as a team.

Serving as pastoral musicians in this era of the church's history is indeed a privilege. Theologically, the challenge of the future revolves around the church's relationship to the world. Music is but one aspect of the whole. But what an important one! Let us feel free to use our gifts to create, to inspire. If in the process of learning to walk we stumble a bit, we need not fear. Sacred music must not be afraid to embrace the twentieth century or the twenty-first century. We as pastoral musicians have the gifts to empower the world for worship.

Robert Strusinski

NINE

SEVEN RULES FOR MAKING IT WORK

More than any other in history, this generation of Roman Catholics is aware of the breadth of diversity of its global communion. The travels of Pope John Paul II have illuminated the cultural differences that encase allegiance to the one Catholic Church. In one form or another, Catholics are faced with the challenge to be true to their own culture on the one hand and the Church Universal on the other. Imagine: bare-bottomed New Guinea natives in flamboyant headdress and body paint processing gifts to the altar accompanied by rhythmic drumming; a seed bed of lay administered "base communities" in Latin America organizing a mission to engage in struggles for social change; Catholic Japanese women forced to marry outside the faith in a country where Catholicism claims less than one percent of the population, presenting offerings before their household shrines and burning incense to honor deceased relatives—an incompatible cultic practice Japanese bishops have just accommodated; and Indian Catholic priests praying and presiding while sitting on the floor like devotees in a Hindu ashram.

The church in this country displays nearly as much dramatic diversity. We need not even invoke the wide range of cultural expressions of Hispanic, Hmong, Black, and Polish to find vastly different understandings of ecclesiology, ministry, and worship. Differences extend not only to territory and culture, but also

within the same parish. In my own diocese, some parishes celebrate liturgies regularly in Latin, some do not allow communion
in the hand, some link hands during the Lord's Prayer, some
stand for the eucharistic prayer, some never sing the responsorial
psalm, and some always sing the Lamb of God. Even within a
single parish Fr. "X" commands the altar boys to ring the bells at
the consecration, and Fr. "Y" will wring their necks if they do.

PLURALISTIC CHARACTER OF THE EARLY CHURCH

The demand for uniformity (and uniforms!) that many of us
were raised on stems from a misconception that the followers of
Jesus lived a life of uniformity and harmony, which, in fact, they
did not. The missionary work of Paul and the social world of
early Christianity give clear indication that the church was not
monolithic but pluralistic, cultural as much as counter-cultural.
"Households" were the basic cell of the mission of the first generations, and it's not surprising that the stage was set for conflict
in beliefs, rituals, degrees of commitment, allocation of power,
and delineation of roles. Clearly, synagogue concepts of community and practice that transferred to the Christian community,
such as circumcision, were met with vehemence by Paul. The
dialectic between structure and antistructure appears again and
again in the tension of Paul's letters. For example, no sooner does
he espouse language of "one body/one spirit" than Paul insists
the male and female prophets, even though they are filled with
the "one spirit" (and even though in Christ there was no more
male/female, Greek/Jew), must keep the different hair styles and
modes of dress customary for men and women.

For a fascinating view of the pluralistic beginnings of the
church, consider the remarkable work by Wayne A. Meeks, *The
First Urban Christians: The Social World of the Apostle Paul*. He says:
"Acts of the Apostles and the Pauline letters provide only tantal-
izing glimpses of the rituals practiced by the Pauline churches,
but these glimpses are only enough to see that they have adopted
or created a rich variety of ceremonial forms. There is a striking
mix of the free and the customary, the familiar and the novel, the
simple and the complex."

It is not by chance that households were the key unit in the early church, that the language of Paul speaks of its members as if they were family: "Children of God, and the apostles, brothers, sisters, beloved." He also speaks frequently and fervently of mutual love through the use of rich emotional language. And finally Paul ascribes a prominent role in the "family" to the spirit and gifts.

Who of us could not look back to a recent holiday gathering of our own families (or someone's we shared) and see a remarkable breadth of diversity of persons, talent, lifestyle, spirituality, and values, and yet deny the fusion of individuals into a unit bound by common love? This spring my family celebrated our parents' fiftieth wedding anniversary . . . of sorts . . . You see, they had their share of upheavals and departures, but then is there anyone who believes a half century of unqualified wedded bliss is really possible? The lives of their five boys (together for the first time in many years) is as varied and colorful as the dynamic of our parental saga. The folks wisely chose to forgo a big extended party and enjoy the weekend with immediate members only. Gathered around a large table with sons and wives or almost wives or significant others, we had the rare chance to sense triumph and wholeness. We not only survived but reached a new place, a new level of integration and identity as a family. The kaleidoscope of campfires, hunting and fishing trips, baseball, macaroni suppers, and booze-brawling skirmishes jelled if only for an instant in this ever-changing collage of memories. And of course, the scenario for our gathering was the meal—the only real chance for us to express our completeness in a common sharing of thanks and joy.

THE NATURE OF COMMUNITY

The intimacy of this togetherness suggests the symbol of community that we all experience on many levels—from Dr. Spock and the family cell to the global synthesis of love and matter envisioned by de Chardin and the eschatological community expressed in Mark (1:15): "This is the time of fulfillment." Community suggests the opposite of disunity. Whereas disunity connotes separation, division, and opposition, community means togetherness, union, and friendship. The word community itself is a rich multi-dimensional symbol not only because of its meaning of unity of persons referring to closeness, personal relations, mutual understanding, common goals and interests, and the like, but because of the concrete reality of diversity and differentiation within community.

In his book, *Community and Disunity*, Abbot Jerome Theisen, O.S.B. offers the explanation that "disunity is caused to a great extend by the lack of will to share the goods of the earth. Individual and corporate greed is at the basis of much suffering and creates a division in the human community." In the same vein I would offer that community is created, strengthened, and nurtured when its members share their gifts. We create community first by naming our needs, accepting our differences, and sharing our diversity of riches.

Let's affirm the positive value of diversity. Some authors point up the need for diversity if a culture is to progress. The same is true for some definitions of social organizations that point to flexibility and diversity as essential elements. T.S. Eliot reflects on diversity and unity in these words: ". . . a people should be neither too united or too divided if its culture is to flourish. Excess of unity may be due to barbarism and may lead to tyranny [God forbid the church be accused of barbaric leadership]; excess of division may be due to decadence and may also lead to tyranny; either excess will prevent preservation or development." Speaking about national cultures Eliot continues: "If it is to flourish [it] should be a constellation of cultures, the constituents of which, benefitting each other, benefit the whole." And Wayne A. Meeks writes: "We find in the letters of Paul a stress on the symbols of unity, equality and love—but also on the correlative symbols of fluidity, diversity and individuation."

Communion in Christ is living a community of belief—a common commitment to the person and word of Jesus. We do not all have the same impression of Jesus or the same commitment, but the range of unity far outreaches the elements of difference. We may be divided on recipes, consistency, and size of the bread, or the hows and whys of the cup, but the message is the same. This broad sharing in the one faith that Paul summed up in the confession "Jesus is Lord" (1 Cor) is a force that overcomes isolation and disunity. And where does this community of God manifest itself? In eucharist and worship, the word and the table. "Is not the cup of blessing we bless a sharing in the blood of Christ?" (1 Cor 10:11). Eucharist becomes, then, the unifying force where we surrender our divisions for the sake of a common approach to the throne of our creator God. And music creates the hospitality and comfort that invite the isolated, united the gathered, and challenge the community to a vision of the kingdom that it is called to embody in the world. By gathering in faith we honor and acknowledge one another's faith. By celebrating what we share as common values, beliefs, and commitments, we also celebrate our differences.

The community gathering for prayer brings with it a vast history of experiences of God and as many reasons for being there. The preoccupied mindsets span from near mesmerized vacuity and boredom to frenzied anxiety or enthusiasm. And it is music with all the transformative, symbolic power of art that can most enliven this spectrum into a common experience of mystery. The nature of art possesses a universality that relates to a diversity and to a flexibility in intention and interpretation. As musicians and planners we persistently mistake our music to mean one thing (fitting one theme) or for performing one particular function. If we plan traveling music to fill some gap—it becomes that and only that.

THE POWER OF MUSIC

Music—regardless of style—has the charge and the integrity of art to be a universal expression of the multiple, the various, the changing. And, as liturgical art, its conception and execution is non-specific and not produced with the intent to serve aesthetic contemplation . . . or to kill time. Like good art and architecture it invites, harbors, and serves our celebrations. Music possesses an aesthetic power of timelessness that breaks down boundaries of the present and the past, and eliminates the contrasts and the tensions of taste and style. The designs of Frank Lloyd Wright, the marvels of Torvill and Dean dancing on ice, and the sleek sculpture of Henry Moore offer a far-reaching avenue of approach to reverence, beauty, and awe. (Amy Grant and born-again Bob Dylan, with all their immensity of message, sweet remoteness, and diverse appeal, lack the inclusive breadth to invoke the transcendent and to suggest a fresh dimension to redemption.)

Successful liturgical music embodies in concrete sound the possibility that redemption means a creative advance to a more poignant, immediate remembrance of the past, or conversely, that the presence of the past transforms the present, giving it richness and depth. Our music, then, gives a new vision in concrete form and calls theology beyond abstract contemplation to action and reality. In other words, music creates the dynamic for change. The implications for us? Genuine artistry. Not pietistic pandering, virtuosic display, or academic swagger . . . or God forbid, ineptitude. Our performance and its intent are not means of *transportation*, to simply take people from one place and return them whence they came through amusement, entertainment, or diversion. They are a means of *transformation*, to take people to a new place and provide the prodding and provocation for permanent change.

PRINCIPLES OR SUGGESTIONS

Having looked at the pluralistic character of the early church, the nature of community and its inherent diversity, and the power of music as symbol to contain and express communion of belief, let me dare to stretch out my neck. Recognizing that I'm mid-stream in the life's work, I'd like to move beyond theory to a framework of principles for making decisions or suggestions for gathering our many parts into an integrated expression of oneness. This list is only a beginning, and we can add or subtract as needs and ideas change.

Respect and Nurture the Gifts of Others.

Let's face it: especially in conflict situations its takes a real effort to look at the positive. But all of us (no matter how wonderful or talented we are, or how much fun we are to be with) are made more complete and effective by pooling resources and affirming the strengths of others and the support they give our work. There is no room for exclusivity or elitism, regardless of our skill level, the extent of our experience, or the medium of our music. We must move beyond a mere tolerance for different styles, values, tastes, and talents to a position of integration and cooperation. We are not Lone Rangers. A guideline from the bishops' Environment and Art in Catholic Worship states: "If we maintain that no human word or art form can contain or exhaust the mystery of God's love . . ." then I think it follows that we must use many expressions—and that means people—and we are the ones to call them, though sometimes they call on us, or we inherit them. One of the first persons I met at my first parish was Bob Gacek, an accordian player who informed me he played his accordian for the 9:00 A.M. Mass when he wasn't "on the road." With honest down-home hospitality his burly, polka pounding hand crushed my dainty baroque-studied digits and I smiled and thought to myself: "Not in my church!" But my concealed arrogance took a whipping. Bob turned out to be an excellent musician and did a masterful job of supporting congregational song by supplementing the limited organ and even accompanying on his own with amplification. I hope I'll never be that quick to jump to judgment again.

A somewhat less affirming case occurred when I asked a former student how she dealt with the pastor in her first year at a parish. She had just related the latest incident about the pastor's impromptu announcement (unbeknownst to her or the ushers) at the end of the "offertory" that they were going to take up a second collection. He motioned over to her at the organ and said: "And let's have a little music during this." Taking some serious issue with the lack of care Father demonstrated for ritual and the function of music, she confronted him after Mass. His response was "I know you're usually right, Mary, but I still like to do things my way." So the lesson Mary consoles herself with is "to deal with differences by not taking things personally." And also, I hope, by having patience and persistence to work for change.

Cultivate Artistry.

I don't think it really matters much what we do, as long as it's done well. The poorest piece of music done well does greater reverence to a community's recognition of the sacred than the greatest piece of music done poorly. The one consistent demand we find threading instructions on music and liturgy is for reverence. Our response must be one of depth of totality, authenticity, genuineness, and care with everything we use and do. A simple attractive beauty is a most effective invitation to seeing beyond the face of individualism to a sense of the holy, the numinous. Anything that kills a spirit of prayer, *reverence*, and a sense of the holy detracts from a sense of unity. We need to be more attentive to how we do it rather than what we do.

There is no want for wonderful repertoire, but I question how much demand there is for the "how to do it." Do we seriously take our responsibility to develop skills, lift our standards, study, practice, belong to professional organizations, sing or play with community or professional ensembles, listen to music—of *all* kinds, and read, *anything*? As artists we need to nourish artistic lives.

Cultivate Variety.

The first axiom for harboring hospitality is the familiar. But it doesn't take long for us to package and pigeonhole our liturgies by saving the diskette and deleting or changing a thing or two in the program each week. Again Environment and Art warns: "Be aware of formulas and patterns which tend to petrify, make manageable and efficient, and which can fail to seek the fullest sense of power and meaning."

I believe "Glory and Praise" is an example of repertoire— whereas it provided a valuable direction and still deserves a viable existence—that has become a victim of misuse. The talents of other good composers are also in danger of overkill leading to an impoverishment of our faith vocabulary. The demand for revitalizing and reevaluating is ever present if we are to combat complacency and a common experience of the boring. In addition to Mass, do we seek opportunities to provide a regular experience and a rich variety of liturgy of the hours and other prayer forms for ourselves and our communities?

Eliminate Diversification of Masses.

Does this sound familiar? "Thank you for calling St. Hilary on the Rocks. Our Mass schedule is as follows:

Sat.	5:15 P.M.	High School Folk Group
Sun.	8:00 A.M.	Silent Mass
	9:15	Organ and Cantor
	10:30	In the Main Church: Adult Choir
	10:30	In the Basement: Contemporary Choir
	12:15 P.M.	The weary Music Director and whomever he or she can find not watching the NFL"

The cultivation and separation of a distinction of Mass styles and repertoire within the same community leads to a diversification, a spreading out of riches, that is counterproductive to community. For one segment of a parish to experience sung prayer from supplements and miscellaneous overhead projections and another only hymns and tremolo (or worse yet, no song) is divisive, dilutes identity, encourages anonymity, and leads to liturgical planning that is arbitrary and confusing. Rather, I think it's possible to use a variety of musical styles and accompaniments that still respect: the faith experience and needs of a multifaceted congregation; strengths and abilities of various musicians; specific demands of particular liturgies relative to time of day, nature, and size of gathering; gifts and person of the presider, etc. The mixture of styles is possible when one understands scale, perspective, design, and intention. In fact, a marriage of art forms like pottery, painting, and sculpture is possible in a single work at the hands of an artist who can make connections and see relationships. Who created the paradigm one pastor is reported to have said: "My job is to make everybody happy!"? No mother with half her faculties would believe that. Planning delicatessen liturgies for folks of different tastes, age, spirituality, and persuasions is like Imelda Marcos shopping for shoes. Studies indicate, furthermore, that of all the reasons people attend a certain liturgy, time of day is the most influential. I know of a downtown city parish that advertises its Sunday morning Mass schedule as "traditional organ/hymns" and the afternoon Masses as "contemporary/folk." For a twist they invert the patterns and feature the contemporary music in the morning and the traditional music in the afternoon "in order that the congregation(s) [within a congregation!] have the opportunity to see how the other people worship"!

Eliminate Multiplicity of Masses.

The Notre Dame study of Catholic parish life points out the needless multiplication of Masses, which results in the deterioration of the quality of worship. Elsewhere, Fr. Robert Hovda points out that you cannot continue to celebrate multiple Mass liturgies that will be inspiring. "Our schedules remain a major obstacle. Instead of gathering believers together, we disperse them. Instead of one or two celebrations into which we pour our time, energy, money, talents, artists, and care with a memorable and inspiring effect, we prefer a half dozen perfunctory, dutiful and depressing rites."

Cultivate a Sense for Good, Sound, Fitting Sung Prayer.

The repertoire in denominational hymnody is a good study of diversity. An interesting look at the struggle is the dynamic of a committee at work in choosing hymnal contents. The United Methodist Hymnal Revision Committee recently encountered the familiar problems with sexist language—and some extra twists such as the American Indians' objection to "pilgrim feet" in "America the Beautiful" and the unfavorable racial connotations to "Whiter Than Snow, Lord Wash Me" and "For our race so freely given" in the hymn "For the Beauty of the Earth," which will become "To the world so freely given." The measure of that diversity is also reflected in a poll throughout their denomination that ranked "How Great Thou Art" and "The Old Rugged Cross" as the two all-time favorites. But the same two hymns also topped the most-hated list. "Onward, Christian Soldiers" was axed because of militaristic overtones until National Headquarters heard over forty thousand complaints about its removal.

One of the strengths of diversity is the implication it holds for ecumenical expression. I feel the current revision of hymnals is doing nearly as much to facilitate the convergence of rites as the implementation of the lectionary. A late eighteenth century English hymn, German "Lutheran" chorales, and a Ghana folk song side by side with "What Is This Place," "Jesus My Lord, My God, My All," and "Gather Us In," as contrasting as they are, all possess the integrity to create hospitality and comfort.

I don't intend to emphasize hymnody over other styles of song, but I think Roman Catholics are in danger of losing a sense of hymnology. And I think hymns, largely due to the expanse of image in their poetry, offer us a wide communion and richness of diversity. The strength of hymns is losing ground because folk music is performed better. The Catholic Church needs more competent organists who can express the music with correct notes, who can phrase and articulate with sensitivity, and lead with strong rhythm and registration. Good organs attract good organists. Hymn singing will always take a back seat to pleasing folk monody and antiphonal song until we experience hymns regularly and effectively.

The sense for good and fitting music is just that: quality and appropriateness. Quality, which is not always immediately appropriate, "has an inherent sense of love, care, honesty and nobility," never compromising, gimmicky, or trivial. Appropriate is "capable of bearing the weight of mystery, awe and reverence," and it must serve the ritual action.

Sing by Heart.

I think the metaphor "Singing by heart" rather than by memory is a metaphor that has something to offer us—for it's the *place of the heart* that is the wellspring of Christian affections: joy, thanks, longing, love, forgiveness. Do we encourage needless reliance on participation aids with printed snippets of melodies and acclamations that perpetuate a missalette mentality? Some common repertoire sung *from the heart* can be a powerful symbol of communion.

* * * *

Where does all this theoretical ramble lead or leave us? I don't know. I promised not to give solutions to these issues, and I'm confident that I am succeeding. One safe conclusion might be that we, who symbolize the living church, value unity over conformity. I think, however, that we can benefit from asking the question—are our expectations for unity too high? Do we expect our ministry to be pie in the sky? There are struggles ahead. But as a people of faith, we embrace the knowledge that unity is born out of struggle and conversion is born out of change. After all, isn't this the heart of the Paschal Mystery—dying and rising— that out of the paralysis of struggle come the freedom and the cure for new life?

The Notre Dame study reveals some depressing things about Catholic parish life and worship in particular. I'd recommend reading the excellent commentary which was given at the North American Academy of Liturgy and published in *Worship* (1986). There's a lot that does not bode well: the dissatisfaction with music in the liturgy is frightening. Some statistics are staggering: only twenty-eight percent of Catholics rate worship of God or celebration of Mass and sacraments the top parish function, and only a small seventeen percent feel that liturgy should be given a higher priority. Nevertheless, we must embrace the challenge to be positive.

In a recent TV interview, a scientist made some comments on the scientific method that I would like to apply to our ministry as artists. He said: "The rewards in scientific research are much greater than the disappointments. Progress is slow and rarely is there a great breakthrough. It's mostly routine, hard work, trying the same thing a lot of different ways, with occasional feedback to know we're on the right track. And care and support for colleagues is a big factor for keeping going."

As pastoral musicians, we live in *different* places, and yet affirm the *same* journey. We show many *different* tastes, but share the *same* thirst. We use many *different* expressions, but share the *same* message. These are enough reasons to stand fast, to face the challenge of our work, and to always give thanks that we are called together to be many parts of one body.

TEN

THE CARE AND FEEDING OF PASTORAL MUSICIANS

Our topic is the nurture, care, and feeding of the pastoral musician. Along the way it will become clear that as we grow ourselves, we become more interested in the growth of those we serve.

But before we begin to consider growth, we need to consider what it is that is to grow. We need to reflect upon the nature of our ministry. We need to attempt a definition of our ministry. One can define our work in so many ways if only because what we do is so complex, so uniquely influenced by the nature of those we serve, and our relationship to those disparate elements. For our purposes here, let's propose that a pastoral musician is one who assists others to encounter God, the Holy One, through the art of music.

As a parish musician, one of the ways I encounter God is through my reading and study of texts. In fact my music making is disciplined by my encounters with text: the weekly appointed Scriptures, the texts of the liturgy, and the texts of hymns. It is a pleasure for me to read these texts and let them rattle around in my brain. To think about them and let my imagination respond to them is a joy as well as a responsibility. For example, let's consider the words of the fifth-century liturgy, the Liturgy of St. James, as translated by Gerald Moultry:

Let all mortal flesh keep silence,
And with fear and trembling stand.

These are wonderful and evocative words, but tell me, do we come to worship expecting to bow in fear and trembling before the Omnipotent One? How about our parishioners? I would venture a guess that most folk have a bit of trouble identifying with the vision Isaiah recalled when he wrote:

> In the year that King Uzziah died I saw the Lord sitting upon a throne, high and lifted up; and his train filled the temple. Above him stood the seraphim; each had six wings: with two he covered his face, and with two he covered his feet, and with two he flew. And one called to another and said: "Holy, holy, holy is the Lord of Hosts; the whole earth is full of his glory." And the foundations of the thresholds shook at the voice of him who called, and the house was filled with smoke.

Ironically, while we may have trouble with it, isn't this vision of an awesome and overwhelming God something that we all seek? It is fundamental to our understanding of God that we sense that God is not one of us. God became one of us but in essence is *God*, not human. We need the holy, we need something to worship and adore, and if we don't find it in our liturgies we will look elsewhere. If God is not special, remote, and mysterious, we create others who are. We do it with movie stars and rock stars. We are in awe of a Streisand or a Redford. It is no accident that such persons are called idols, false gods created to take the place of the true God, whom many have stripped of holiness and mystery. The quest for the holy is essential for the human spirit. If we remove it from our faith life, it springs up elsewhere. Teilhard de Chardin speaks for me and I hope for you, when he says:

> What I cry out for, with my whole life and all my earthly passion, is something very different from an equal to cherish; it is a God to adore. To adore . . . that means to lose oneself in the unfathomable, to plunge into the inexhaustible, to find peace in the incorruptible, to be absorbed in defined immensity, to offer oneself to the fire and the transparency.

For me this holy should be a part of our worship. And if we are to experience this holy, not simply an equal to cherish but a God to adore, one thing is required of us in preparation. Remember the story in Exodus of the meeting of God with Israel at Mount Sinai. God instructed Moses, "Go to the people and consecrate them today and tomorrow and let them wash their garments and be ready for the third day, for on the third day the Lord will come down on Mount Sinai in the sight of all the people." The people were to prepare for their encounter with God; the God of majesty and power, the Holy One.

I wonder if we can expect to encounter this holy God without preparing ourselves. It is interesting to note that to this day Orthodox Jews make careful preparations for the sabbath, knowing that such readying gives their worship on the sabbath more meaning. I'm sure that each of us feels that we do prepare ourselves to fill our responsibilities at worship. I'm sure that the hymns are practiced and the homilies are thought out. We do well with this week to week preparation, but we also need a different kind of preparation—the long-term nurturing that is essential to support our weekly work of worship leadership. We are like a well that is fed by a spring; if the spring goes dry, the well goes dry as well. Yet so often we are caught up, legitimately so, in our work of worship planning, rehearsing, leading, that we are in danger of running dry as the time for our personal growth gets shortchanged. In that context—the need for time for personal growth—I'd like to consider our needs for three kinds of time: up time, down time, and reflection time.

Up Time

Up time is for continuing education. Continuing education is not the thing that you do for three days each summer. It is much more than that. It is Bible study, reading about liturgies, study of hymnology, theological study, and especially the continuing study of music. In *Gravity and Grace*,[1] a new book from Augsburg Publishing House, the distinguished theologian Joseph Sitler writes of his disappointment upon visiting former students now in the ministry and seeing no signs, no evidence of any concern for continuing growth. I wonder how many music teachers might write the same thing about their former students?

In your work, what areas do you feel a bit unsure about: areas that might go a little better with additional information to help support the work? Consider making a list of these areas and search for resources, ways to enable a bit of growth. Perhaps even more importantly, what areas do you feel *good* about that should be probed more deeply? Just between us musicians, tell me "How's your practice life?" The great French organist Marcel Dupré once observed that he liked two hours of piano practice before beginning his daily organ practice. That's incomprehensible to me. I can't imagine the luxury of two hours to *get ready* to practice. We must find time for disciplined practice. This does not include just the work on hymns for next week or work on any voluntaries—preludes and postludes needed. Rather, it might be basic technical studies or time for work on a new piece to expand the repertoire, to grow.

We also grow by listening to music. Do you go to concerts, orchestra concerts, chamber music recitals, choir concerts, and of course, organ recitals? And when you go to a concert, are you an active or a passive listener? In *Gravity and Grace* Joseph Sitler has something to say about an active, not passive approach to growth.

> Growth in the life of the mind, a lifelong deepening of reflection, may sometimes begin in awkward hesitation—or equally, in the examination of snappy opinions. If I continue throughout my life to regard with ever-renewed admiration a Rembrandt self-portrait, my mind is not enriched by ever more vehement statements of my admiration. One must, rather, keep pushing the question, "What is admirable about the admirable?" We really do not get to know one another by exchanging catalogs of likes and dislikes. Real understanding grows with probing.

Of course we need to set aside a week or two for continuing educational experiences. But what about time during the year? Do we take time during the year to nurture our art? How about some private study this year? We all need it.

And what about theological and spiritual growth? We need to give attention to these areas just as much as we need to tend to our musical growth. A basic, disciplined study of the appointed texts for each week could be a very good beginning for probing deeper, growing, and enriching the wellsprings of understanding from which we make pastoral music.

Then, as pastoral musicians, we need to remember one other area. Because of our responsibilities as worship leaders we rarely get to be a person in the pew. From time to time we need to be just that, not only to experience what it's like out there in the real world, but also to be freed from our obligations as leaders, freed to involve ourselves totally in the discipline of prayer. For each of us this worship time, time when we really *just worship*, is of the utmost necessity and must be found. Each of us will find a different way to do this; it is an essential part of our nurture.

Reflection Time

I consider reflection time just as essential for our nurture and growth. Each of us needs to find a quiet place away from distractions, a place to be alone and at peace. We can have prayer and meditation in these places, and we can reflect upon the Bible study that we might be doing, or we could just sit, letting our imaginations roam freely, leading us to new ideas for way to do a specific hymns, a liturgy for a specific feast day, or whatever. And there, most importantly, we can give the Spirit time to do its work with us. How long has it been since we've heard an angel sing? We need to find a quiet place, a place quiet enough that maybe just once in our very busy lives we might be blessed to hear an angel sing.

Down Time

We also need down time. Time for reflection is not down time. Down time is your own time when you do something not at all related to your usual work. Down time is when you indulge your secret or not so secret vice. (For me it's reading detective stories or tinkering with my 1952 classic Jeep). When engrossed in one's secret vice, there is no time for thinking about one's work. And that's good!

When it comes to down time, my guess is that most of you are like me. There is never enough time for down time. One of my concerns as I observe and dialogue with pastoral musicians is that many are much too busy. We do need to be careful about being overloaded. If we try to do too much, nothing is done well.

Keep a careful eye on your workload and keep raising this issue in the appropriate places until a realistic workload is evolved. No one can play all the weekend liturgies, do a wedding or two, lead all the choirs, and teach in the school for long without totally depleting themselves of their creative energies. Even if one can physically keep up the pace, it is impossible to maintain the levels of creative energy required to do all these things well. Remember that it is in the best interest of the people you serve that you not be overworked. They deserve and should have the best you can offer, not the work of an exhausted, artistically drained person. Do remember that we ultimately *do* have control over being exploited. We can say no. It is often hard to say no because we feel that if we refuse to do something, it won't get done. But sometimes that's just as well, since when we are overworked, things often go wrong. It is imperative to learn our limits and learn to say no.

Inducing Growth

I've been speaking of the need for energy, creative energy, physical energy that comes from having been renewed and relaxed in order to offer our best. But what is it that we do? What is it that we offer to our congregations as pastoral musicians? What is our responsibility to these people with whom we worship weekly? Part of our responsibility is a concern for the growth of our congregations. Just as we need to be concerned about our own growth and nurture, as pastoral musicians we have a responsibility to nurture those we serve, especially to nurture the quality of the worship life of the congregation we serve. I am concerned that we are shortchanging our people and stunting their growth.

So we try to induce growth, encourage change, and then we get complaints. "I tried to get the congregation more involved in singing, and some members got so upset that they called a special meeting of the parish board . . ." Was the soil prepared? Were people informed about the changes to be made? Was the seed planted well? Was the new material taught well? Was time allowed for the crop to grow? How about the patience factor? It takes time for the crop to grow, for change to be accepted. And always, always remember that by and large only the dissatisfied speak out.

What about quality? For me, great art, timeless art, is the most appropriate art to support and enrich our worship life. Now by great art I do not mean something that is invariably complicated or involved. But, on the other hand, great art is something that is not totally accessible on first encounter. A very wise person once observed that if something can be understood totally upon first encounter, it probably doesn't deserve to endure. The Gospel, the story of the good news of our redemption in Jesus Christ, is great art. It is a story immediately simple and yet very profound. A lifetime of study is not enough for someone who really wishes to understand the total implications of this incredible good news that we call the Gospel. Why is it then, that we are afraid of great art, great music, to complement and support this great story? Great art is also immediately simple in that a part of its message is clear from the first. But, like the Gospel, continued study can increase one's understanding and appreciation.

The Servant Role

Much has been said about the pastoral musician as a servant. We are servants of the people but need to be very careful about our understanding of the implications of that servant role. Dorothy Sayers created a detective named Lord Peter Wimsey, one of those typical, incredibly wealthy English lords who really don't need to work for a living. In the first of the Wimsey adventures, Sayers introduces the major characters in situations that clarify their relationships to each other. One important character is Bunter, Peter's butler and gentlemen's gentleman. Wimsey has been out for a busy morning of detecting and returns home at noon in great haste to get a catalog for a book auction he wishes to attend. Bunter gives him the catalog but blocks the door. "My lord, you are improperly dressed to go to the auction. Your clothing has been laid out on the bed." "Bunter, Bunter, I'm late. I must go!" "My lord, dress." And so Wimsey rushes down the hall to his room, and changes clothes muttering, "Bunter, Bunter, what would I do without you?" Yes, we need to have the courage to prod, to guide, to encourage, not just passively respond to what the people think they want.

One reason it is so important to understand our servant role in relation to the people we serve is that we have another, more important servant role. We are servants of the word, God's word.

We have a story to tell, and what an incredible story it is. The arts are one of the best storytelling devices available to us. We need not be afraid of the challenge of great art in this context. Let me quote again from *Gravity and Grace*.

> In the uses of literature, the uses of art, I find our intellectual obligation being unfulfilled. We simply are not cultivated people in our time. Of the old church an ancient historian said: "The church in the first three centuries won the empire because it out-lived, outthought, and it outdid the pagan world"—including intellectual and artistic achievement. But much of the intellectual and aesthetic life within the contemporary congregation is simply contemptible. It is often full of moral fervor and piety, but it is usually absent in the clarity of ideas that thread against the accepted norms and offer new possibilities for reflection.
>
> How is it possible that our church social room should be filled with pictures that are mostly *Kitsch*, to use that eloquent German word, when centuries of artists have taken religious symbols and given them eloquent expression? I am continually amazed by the fact that something happens when one becomes pious. Is the price of piety stupidity? Is the result of being devout that one becomes intellectually and aesthetically insensitive so that the actualities of this world are no longer available to us?

In this context I would like to rewrite one hymn text:

Now thank we all our God
With heart and hands and voices.

Let's change that as follows:

Now thank we all our God
With heart, head, hands and voices.

Or as Sitler would observe, "It's not necessary to have a cranial bypass to be a Christian."

It is terribly important to provide a ministry of music that is sensitive and caring, yet utilizing material of intellectual and aesthetic worth. What do we serve at our weekly eucharistic banquets? Artistic pabulum in many cases. When you are invited for thanksgiving dinner, you expect a feast, not hot dogs. "But my people aren't ready for it." Get them to try it. They'll like it— eventually. It's a bit like encouraging a child to expand the palate, grow beyond pizza and hamburgers. This is where the "pastoral" part of pastoral musician comes to the fore. The trying must be done with tender loving care and great patience. I'm interested in slow growth. I'm thinking about five years from now, not five weeks. But the growing begins with next week.

Now it is important to be clear about one thing. In encouraging growth and expressing a concern for the quality of what we do, I don't mean to imply that all we do must be complex or difficult. A great folk melody is wonderfully simple yet remarkably profound. A great text challenges us to encounter it tomorrow and the day after tomorrow as well as today. My interest is to challenge our people to do their very best on the literature we do use while being sure to provide for new things that are ever better, ever richer evocations of our faith. Growth is essentially change. Luther said it this way:

> You should not imagine that the life of a Christian is something stationary and inactive. On the contrary, it is a transition and a progress and do not consider someone a Christian who is not engaged in transition. For this life is not a being, but a becoming. It is not a being holy but a becoming holy. It is not being well, but a getting well. Not cleanliness but cleansing. This life is a journey in which we constantly progress and yet are not what we ought to be.

Growth, change, becoming . . . this is what I have been considering. To begin, I proposed a definition of the pastoral musician as one who assists others into a better understanding of God, the Holy One, through the art, the language of music.

Second, I have proposed that in order to be equipped for this ministry we need to be concerned about our own personal nurture and growth. We need up time: learning time, practice time, study time. We need reflection time: time to process what we have learned, time to let our imagination have free rein, time to let the Holy Spirit be our leaven. And we need down time: time away from our work to insure that as we return to our work, we return refreshed.

Third, we need to be intentional in our planning for, our concern for, our care for the growth of the people we serve. Their spiritual growth, as well as the growth of their worship life, is something for which we need to take at least some responsibility.

And it is my conviction that this growth cannot occur without working to raise the theological and musical integrity and quality of what we do.

St. Olaf College, where I teach, is a college of the American Lutheran Church and to date most of my students have been Protestant. I tell them that if I could do it over again, start all over, I would love to serve a Roman Catholic parish and that they should consider this option as well. You are living in and you are a part of a revolution, a reforming of what you do, that is shaking and shaping the Roman Catholic Church in vital new ways. What a special and frustrating yet so very exciting time in which to be a pastoral musician. There is great cause for hope in what we are doing. Things are moving in the right direction. It is our high calling to claim the beyond, to move forward, to probe deeper, to work to sing the Lord's song in ever richer and more vital ways.

Note

1. Excerpts are reprinted by permission from *Gravity and Grace,* by Joseph Sitler. Copyright © 1986, Augsburg Publishing House, Minneapolis, MN.